Granger Index

5/15/80 #8

POEMS BY GRADES

GRAMMAR

POEMS BY GRADES

CONTAINING

POEMS SELECTED FOR EACH GRADE OF THE
SCHOOL COURSE, POEMS FOR EACH
MONTH AND MEMORY GEMS

BY

ADA VAN STONE HARRIS

AND

CHARLES B. GILBERT

VOL. II

FOR GRADES 5, 6, 7, 8

Granger Index Reprint Series

BOOKS FOR LIBRARIES PRESS
FREEPORT, NEW YORK

First Published 1907
Reprinted 1971

INTERNATIONAL STANDARD BOOK NUMBER:
0-8369-6228-1

LIBRARY OF CONGRESS CATALOG CARD NUMBER:
78-149103

PRINTED IN THE UNITED STATES OF AMERICA

PREFACE

THESE little books are dedicated to the most useful body of people in the world,—the teachers. They are sent forth in the hope that they may at least " push a pound," and by so much lighten the burden of some soul toiling for the children.

A very general and eminently proper demand of courses of study is for the use of much literature, especially poems, in all the grades, and teachers often experience great difficulty in finding appropriate material that has not been already studied in some lower grades.

The kindergartners and the teachers of the earlier primary grades cull the available literature and often leave little for the teacher of the higher grades, with which she is familiar. Hence results much repetition and consequent loss of interest. Sometimes, too, it is to be feared that teachers in their desperation use selections that cannot properly be called good literature.

The compilers of these books have endeavored to help over these hard places by supplying, in the first place, an abundance of material, all good and from standard authors, and, in the second place, by grading it, giving to each grade more than can possibly be used, and thus removing

PREFACE

the temptation to take what is better adapted to some other grade.

Features of the books also are the selections for the different seasons and for special occasions and the briefer quotations for memorizing.

The books are the product of experience. If they increase the joys of teaching for any teacher, they will have paid for the making.

CONTENTS

FIFTH YEAR

TITLE	AUTHOR	PAGE
A Christmas Carol	*James Russell Lowell*	3
A Psalm of Life	*Henry W. Longfellow*	5
A Sea Dirge	*Shakespeare*	7
A Song of the Sea	*Bryan Waller Procter (Barry Cornwall)*	8
A Wren's Nest	*William Wordsworth*	10
Evening	*Sir Walter Scott*	14
Excelsior	*Henry W. Longfellow*	15
The Ivy Green	*Charles Dickens*	17
The Old Clock on the Stairs	*Henry W. Longfellow*	19
O Mary, Go and Call the Cattle Home	*Charles Kingsley*	21
Romance of the Swan's Nest	*Elizabeth B. Browning*	22
See What a Lovely Shell	*Alfred Tennyson*	26
The Arrow and the Song	*Henry W. Longfellow*	28
The Ballad of the Boat	*Richard Garnett*	29
The Battle of Blenheim	*Robert Southey*	31
The Day Is Done	*Henry W. Longfellow*	34
The Gladness of Nature	*William C. Bryant*	36
The Housekeeper	*Charles Lamb*	37
The Landing of the Pilgrim Fathers in New England	*Felicia D. Hemans*	38

CONTENTS

TITLE	AUTHOR	PAGE
THE PET LAMB	William Wordsworth	40
THE PLANTING OF THE APPLE TREE	William C. Bryant	44
THE THREE FISHERS	Charles Kingsley	48
THE WRECK OF THE HESPERUS	Henry W. Longfellow	49
THE YELLOW VIOLET	William C. Bryant	53
TO-DAY	Thomas Carlyle	55
TO THE DAISY	William Wordsworth	56
TO THE FRINGED GENTIAN	William C. Bryant	59
UNDER THE GREENWOOD TREE	Shakespeare	60
WOODMAN, SPARE THAT TREE	George P. Morris	61
HOME, SWEET HOME	John Howard Payne	63
LULLABY FOR TITANIA	Shakespeare	64
THE BLUE JAY	Susan Hartley Sweet	66

SIXTH YEAR

THE FLAG GOES BY	Henry H. Bennett	71
ABOU BEN ADEM	Leigh Hunt	73
THE COMING OF SPRING	Nora Perry	74
BURIAL OF SIR JOHN MOORE	Charles Wolfe	76
CHRISTMAS BELLS	Henry W. Longfellow	78
EXILE OF ERIN	Thomas Campbell	80
FOR A' THAT AND A' THAT	Robert Burns	82
"HOW THEY BROUGHT THE GOOD NEWS FROM GHENT TO AIX"	Robert Browning	84
I REMEMBER, I REMEMBER	Thomas Hood	87
KING SOLOMON AND THE ANTS	John G. Whittier	89
LADY CLARE	Alfred Tennyson	92
MY HEART'S IN THE HIGHLANDS	Robert Burns	96
ONE BY ONE	Adelaide A. Procter	97

CONTENTS

TITLE	AUTHOR	PAGE
ORPHEUS WITH HIS LUTE	Shakespeare	99
QUIET WORK	Matthew Arnold	100
REBECCA'S HYMN	Sir Walter Scott	101
REST	Goethe	103
RUTH	Thomas Hood	104
THE BRIDGE	Henry W. Longfellow	105
THE BUILDERS	Henry W. Longfellow	108
THE DESTRUCTION OF SENNACH-ERIB	Lord Byron	110
THE DROVERS	John G. Whittier	112
THE HURRICANE	William C. Bryant	116
THE HERITAGE	James Russell Lowell	118
THE MARSEILLAISE	Rouget de L'Isle	121
THE MINSTREL BOY	Thomas Moore	123
THE NECKAN	Matthew Arnold	124
THE SONG OF THE SHIRT	Thomas Hood	127
THE SPACIOUS FIRMAMENT ON HIGH	Joseph Addison	131
THE WATCH ON THE RHINE	Max Schneckenburger	132
THE WHITE-FOOTED DEER	William C. Bryant	134
MERCY	Shakespeare	138
PUCK AND THE FAIRY QUEEN	Shakespeare	139
MAY	F. D. Sherman	140

SEVENTH YEAR

THE NAME OF OLD GLORY	James W. Riley	143
JOG ON, JOG ON		146
A SONG OF CLOVER	"Saxe Holm".	147
A SONG OF LOVE	Lewis Carroll	148
SCYTHE SONG	Andrew Lang	150

CONTENTS

TITLE	AUTHOR	PAGE
An Interview With Miles Standish	James Russell Lowell	151
Bannockburn	Robert Burns	157
Fidelity	William Wordsworth	159
Good Name in Man and Woman	Shakespeare	162
Hohenlinden	Thomas Campbell	163
Hymn to the North Star	William C. Bryant	165
Thanatopsis	William C. Bryant	167
The Antiquity of Freedom	William C. Bryant	170
The Battle of the Baltic	Thomas Campbell	171
The Cavalry Charge	Edmund C. Stedman	137
The Charge of the Light Brigade	Alfred Tennyson	174
The Crowded Street	William C. Bryant	177
The Finding of the Lyre	James Russell Lowell	179
The Noble Nature	Ben Jonson	181
The Patriot	Robert Browning	182
The Rainy Day	Henry W. Longfellow	184
To a Waterfowl	William C. Bryant	185
The Yankee Girl	John G. Whittier	187
The Pageant	Shakespeare	189
While Shepherds Watched Their Flocks by Night	Nahum Tate	190
Wolsey's Fall	Shakespeare	192

EIGHTH YEAR

The Angler's Reveille	Henry van Dyke	195
Bugle Song	Alfred Tennyson	199
A Farewell	Alfred Tennyson	200

CONTENTS

TITLE	AUTHOR	PAGE
A Forest Hymn	William C. Bryant	201
Alice Brand	Sir Walter Scott	206
Antony's Eulogy on Cæsar	Shakespeare	211
An Order for a Picture	Alice Cary	217
The Bells	Edgar Allan Poe	221
Each and All	Ralph W. Emerson	226
Elegy Written in a Country Church-yard	Thomas Gray	228
Lochinvar	Sir Walter Scott	234
Breathes There the Man	Sir Walter Scott	236
On His Blindness	Milton	237
On the Receipt of My Mother's Picture	William Cowper	238
Polonius' Advice	Shakespeare	243
Recessional	Rudyard Kipling	245
Sir Galahad	Alfred Tennyson	247
Sound the Loud Timbrel	Thomas Moore	251
St. Agnes Eve	Alfred Tennyson	252
The Angels of Buena Vista	John G. Whittier	254
The Awakening of Spring	Alfred Tennyson	259
The Building of the Ship	Henry W. Longfellow	260
The Chambered Nautilus	Oliver W. Holmes	263
The Cloud	Percy B. Shelley	265
The Last Leaf	Oliver W. Holmes	267
The Rainbow	William Wordsworth	269
The Royal George	William Cowper	270
To a Skylark	Percy B. Shelley	272
Waterloo	Lord Byron	277

CONTENTS

PATRIOTIC FOR ALL GRADES

TITLE	AUTHOR	PAGE
HAIL! COLUMBIA	*Joseph Hopkinson*	283
THE AMERICAN FLAG	*Joseph R. Drake*	285
A SONG OF THE CAMP	*Bayard Taylor*	288
BARBARA FRIETCHIE	*John G. Whittier*	290
CONCORD HYMN	*Ralph W. Emerson*	293
NATHAN HALE	*Francis M. Finch*	294
OLD IRONSIDES	*Oliver W. Holmes*	297
SOLDIER, REST!	*Walter Scott*	298
SONG OF MARION'S MEN	*William C. Bryant*	300
THE BLUE AND THE GRAY	*Francis M. Finch*	303
THE RISING IN 1776	*T. Buchanan Read*	306
THE STAR-SPANGLED BANNER	*Francis Scott Key*	310
WAR-SONG	*James G. Percival*	312
WARREN'S ADDRESS	*John Pierpont*	313

QUOTATIONS

MEMORY GEMS (Fifth Grade)		317
MEMORY GEMS (Sixth Grade)		324
MEMORY GEMS (Seventh Grade)		331
MEMORY GEMS (Eighth Grade)		339

FIFTH YEAR

A CHRISTMAS CAROL

"WHAT means this glory round our feet,"
    The Magi mused, " more bright than morn ? "
And voices chanted clear and sweet,
    " Today the Prince of Peace is born! "

" What means that star," the shepherds said,
    " That brightens through the rocky glen ? "
And angels answering overhead,
    Sang, " Peace on earth, good-will to men! "

'Tis eighteen hundred years and more
    Since those sweet oracles were dumb;
We wait for Him, like them of yore;
    Alas, he seems so slow to come!

But it was said in words of gold
    No time or sorrow e'er shall dim,
That little children might be bold
    In perfect trust to come to Him.

All round about our feet shall shine
    A light like that the wise men saw,
If we our loving wills incline
    To that sweet Life that is the Law.

So shall we learn to understand
　The simple faith of shepherds then,
And, clasping kindly hand in hand,
　Sing, " Peace on earth, good-will to men! "

And they who do their souls no wrong,
　But keep at eve the faith of morn,
Shall daily hear the angel-song,
　" Today the Prince of Peace is born! "

JAMES RUSSELL LOWELL.

A PSALM OF LIFE

What the heart of the young man said to the psalmist.

TELL me not in mournful numbers,
　Life is but an empty dream—
For the soul is dead that slumbers,
　And things are not what they seem.

Life is real! Life is earnest!
　And the grave is not its goal;
Dust thou art, to dust returnest,
　Was not spoken of the soul.

Not enjoyment, and not sorrow,
　Is our destined end or way;
But to act that each to-morrow
　Find us farther than today.

Art is long, and Time is fleeting,
　And our hearts, though stout and brave,
Still, like muffled drums are beating
　Funeral marches to the grave.

In the world's broad field of battle,
　In the bivouac of Life,
Be not like dumb, driven cattle!
　Be a hero in the strife!

A PSALM OF LIFE

Trust no Future, howe'er pleasant!
  Let the dead Past bury its dead!
Act,—act in the living Present!
  Heart within, and God o'erhead!

Lives of great men all remind us
  We can make our lives sublime,
And, departing, leave behind us
  Footprints on the sands of time;

Footprints, that perhaps another,
  Sailing o'er life's solemn main,
A forlorn and shipwrecked brother,
  Seeing, shall take heart again.

Let us, then, be up and doing,
  With a heart for any fate;
Still achieving, still pursuing,
  Learn to labor and to wait.

LONGFELLOW.

A SEA DIRGE

[From *The Tempest*.]

FULL fathom five thy father lies;
　Of his bones are coral made;
Those are pearls that were his eyes:
　Nothing of him that doth fade,
But doth suffer a sea-change
Into something rich and strange.
Sea-nymphs hourly ring his knell:
Hark! now I hear them,—ding-dong, bell.

SHAKESPEARE.

A SONG OF THE SEA

THE sea! the sea! the open sea!
 The blue, the fresh, the ever free!
Without a mark, without a bound,
It runneth the earth's wide regions round;
It plays with the clouds; it mocks the skies,
Or like a cradled creature lies.

I'm on the sea! I'm on the sea!
I am where I would ever be;
With the blue above, and the blue below,
And silence whereso'er I go;
If a storm should come and awake the deep,
What matter? I should ride and sleep.

I love (Oh! how I love) to ride
On the fierce, foaming, bursting tide,
When every mad wave drowns the moon,
Or whistles aloft his tempest tune,
And tells how goeth the world below,
And why the southwest blasts do blow.

I never was on the dull tame shore,
But I loved the great sea more and more,
And backwards flew to her billowy breast,
Like a bird that seeketh its mother's nest;
And a mother she was and is to me;
For I was born on the open sea!

8

A SONG OF THE SEA

The waves were white, and red the morn,
In the noisy hour when I was born;
And the whale it whistled, the porpoise rolled,
And the dolphins bared their backs of gold;
And never was heard such an outcry wild
As welcomed to life the ocean child!

I've lived since then, in calm and strife,
Full fifty summers a sailor's life,
With wealth to spend, and power to range,
But never have sought nor sighed for change;
And Death, whenever he come to me,
Shall come on the wide unbounded sea!

BRYAN WALLER PROCTER (*Barry Cornwall*).

A WREN'S NEST

AMONG the dwellings framed by birds
    In field or forest with nice care,
Is none that with the little wren's
    In snugness may compare.

No door the tenement requires,
    And seldom needs a labored roof;
Yet is it to the fiercest sun
    Impervious and storm-proof.

So warm, so beautiful withal,
    In perfect fitness for its aim,
That to the kind by special grace,
    There instinct surely came.

And when for their abodes they seek
    An opportune recess,
The hermit has no finer eye
    For shadowy quietness.

These find, 'mid ivied abbey walls,
    A canopy in some still nook;
Others are pent-housed by a brae
    That overhangs a brook.

There to the brooding bird her mate
  Warbles by fits his low, clear song;
And by the busy streamlet both
  Are sung to all day long.

Or in sequestered lanes they build,
  Where, till the flitting bird's return,
Her eggs within the nest repose,
  Like relics in an urn.

But still, where general choice is good,
  There is a better and a best;
And, among fairest objects, some
  Are fairer than the rest;

This, one of those small builders proved
  In a green covert, where, from out
The forehead of a pollard oak,
  The leafy antlers sprout;

For she had planned the mossy lodge,
  Mistrusting her evasive skill,
Had to a primrose looked for aid
  Her wishes to fulfill.

High on the trunk's projecting brow,
  And fixed an infant's span above
The budding flowers, peeped forth the nest,
  The prettiest of the grove!

The treasure proudly did I show
  To some whose minds without disdain
Can turn to little things; but once
  Looked up for it in vain:

'Tis gone—a ruthless spoiler's prey,
  Who heeds not beauty, love, or song,
'Tis gone (so seemed it)! and we grieved
  Indignant at the wrong.

Just three days after, passing by,
  In clearer light the moss-built cell
I saw, espied its shaded mouth;
  And felt that all was well.

The primrose for a veil had spread
  The largest of her upright leaves;
And thus for purposes benign,
  A simple flower deceives.

Concealed from friends who might disturb
  Thy quiet with no ill intent,
Secure from evil eyes and hands
  On barbarous plunder bent.

Rest, mother bird! and when thy young
  Take flight, and thou art free to roam,
When withered is the guardian flower,
  And empty thy late home,

Think how ye prospered, thou and thine,
  Amid the unviolated grove,
Housed near the growing primrose tuft
  In foresight, or in love.

WORDSWORTH.

EVENING

THE sun upon the lake is low,
    The wild birds hush their song;
The hills have evening's deepest glow,
    Yet Leonard tarries long.
Now, all whom varied toil and care
    From home and love divide,
In the calm sunset may repair
    Each to the loved one's side.

The noble dame on turret high,
    Who waits her gallant knight,
Looks to the western beam to spy
    The flash of armor bright.
The village maid, with hand on brow
    The level ray to shade,
Upon the footpath watches now
    For Colin's darkening plaid.

Now to their mates the wild swans row,
    By day they swam apart;
And to the thicket wanders slow
    The hind beside the hart.
The woodlark at his partner's side
    Twitters his closing song—
All meet whom day and care divide,—
    But Leonard tarries long!

SIR WALTER SCOTT.

EXCELSIOR

THE shades of night were falling fast,
    As through an Alpine village passed
A youth, who bore, 'mid snow and ice,
A banner with the strange device,
          Excelsior!

His brow was sad; his eyes beneath
Flashed like a falchion from its sheath,
And like a silver clarion rung
The accents of that unknown tongue,
          Excelsior!

In happy homes he saw the light
Of household fires gleam warm and bright;
Above, the spectral glaciers shone,
And from his lips escaped a groan,
          Excelsior!

" Try not the Pass! " the old man said;
" Dark lowers the tempest overhead,
The roaring torrent is deep and wide! "
And loud that clarion voice replied,
          Excelsior!

"Oh, stay," the maiden said, "and rest
Thy weary head upon this breast!"
A tear stood in his bright blue eye,
But still he answered, with a sigh,
        Excelsior!

"Beware the pine tree's withered branch,
Beware the awful avalanche!"
This was the peasant's last good-night,
A voice replied far up the height,
        Excelsior!

At break of day as heavenward
The pious monks of St. Bernard
Uttered the oft-repeated prayer,
A voice cried through the startled air,
        Excelsior!

A traveller, by the faithful hound,
Half-buried in the snow was found,
Still grasping in his hand of ice
That banner with the strange device,
        Excelsior!

There in the twilight cold and gray,
Lifeless, but beautiful, he lay,
And from the sky, serene and far,
A voice fell, like a falling star,
        Excelsior!

                LONGFELLOW.

THE IVY GREEN

O H, a dainty plant is the ivy green,
   That creepeth o'er ruins old!
On right choice food are his meals, I ween,
   In his cell so lone and cold.
The walls must be crumbled, the stones decayed,
   To pleasure his dainty whim;
And the mouldering dust that the years have made,
   Is a merry meal for him.
Creeping where no life is seen,
A rare old plant is the ivy green.

Fast he stealeth on, though he wears no wings,
   And a staunch old heart has he;
How closely he twineth, how tight he clings
   To his friend the huge oak-tree!
And shyly he twineth along the ground,
   And his leaves he gently waves;
And he joyously twines and hugs around
   The rich mould of dead men's graves.
Creeping where grim death has been,
A rare old plant is the ivy green.

Whole ages have fled, and their works decayed,
   And nations have scattered been;
But the stout old ivy shall never fade
   From its hale and hearty green.

The brave old plant in its lonely days
   Shall fatten on the past;
For the stateliest building man can raise
   Is the ivy's food at last.
Creeping on where time has been,
A rare old plant is the ivy green.

CHARLES DICKENS.

THE OLD CLOCK ON THE STAIRS

SOMEWHAT back from the village street
  Stands the old-fashioned country seat,
Across its antique portico
Tall poplar trees their shadows throw.
And from its station in the hall
An antique time-piece says to all,—
      " Forever—never!
      Never—forever! "

Half-way up the stairs it stands,
And points and beckons with its hands
From its case of massive oak,
Like a monk who, under his cloak,
Crosses himself, and sighs alas!
With sorrowful voice to all who pass,—
      " Forever—never!
      Never—forever! "

By day its voice is low and light;
But in the silent dead of night,
Distinct as a passing footstep's fall,
It echoes along the vacant hall,
Along the ceiling, along the floor,
And seems to say at each chamber door,—
      " Forever—never!
      Never—forever! "

Through days of sorrow and of mirth,
Through days of death and days of birth
Through every swift vicissitude
Of changeful time, unchanged it has stood,
And as if, like God, it all things saw,
It calmly repeats those words of awe,—
      " Forever—never!
      Never—forever! "

In that mansion used to be
Free-hearted Hospitality;
His great fires up the chimney roared;
The stranger feasted at his board;
But, like the skeleton at the feast,
That warning time-piece never ceased,—
      " Forever—never!
      Never—forever! "

There groups of merry children played,
There youths and maidens dreaming strayed;
O precious hours! O golden prime,
And affluence of love and time!
Even as a miser counts his gold,
Those hours the ancient time-piece told,-
      " Forever—never!
      Never—forever! "

                    LONGFELLOW.

O MARY, GO AND CALL THE CATTLE HOME

O MARY, go and call the cattle home,
      And call the cattle home,
      And call the cattle home,
      Across the sands o' Dee!"
The western wind was wild and dank wi' foam,
      And all alone went she.

The creeping tide came up along the sand,
      And o'er and o'er the sand,
      And round and round the sand,
      As far as eye could see;
The blinding mist came down and hid the land:
      And never home came she.

" Oh, is it weed, or fish, or floating hair,—
      A tress o' golden hair,—
      O' drowned maiden's hair,—
      Above the nets at sea?
Was never salmon yet that shone so fair,
      Among the stakes on Dee."

They rowed her in across the rolling foam,—
      The cruel, crawling foam,—
      The cruel, hungry foam,—
      To her grave beside the sea:
But still the boatmen hear her call the cattle home
      Across the sands o' Dee.

CHARLES KINGSLEY.

ROMANCE OF THE SWAN'S NEST

LITTLE Ellie sits alone
   'Mid the beeches of the meadow,
By a stream-side on the grass;
And the trees are showering down
Doubles of their leaves in shadow,
   On her shining hair and face.

She has thrown her bonnet by;
And her feet she has been dipping
   In the shallow water's flow.
Now she holds them nakedly
In her hands all sleek and dripping,
   While she rocketh to and fro.

Little Ellie sits alone,
And the smile she softly uses,
   Fills the silence like a speech;
While she thinks what shall be done,—
And the sweetest pleasure chooses
   For her future within reach.

Little Ellie in her smile
Chooses, " I will have a lover,
   Riding on a steed of steeds!
He shall love me without guile;
And to him I will discover
   That swan's nest among the reeds.

" And the steed shall be red-roan,
And the lover shall be noble,
With an eye that takes the breath;
And the lute he plays upon
Shall strike ladies into trouble,
As his sword strikes men to death!

" And the steed it shall be shod
All in silver, housed in azure,
And the mane shall swim the wind;
And the hoofs along the sod,
Shall flash onward and keep measure,
Till the shepherds look behind.

" But my lover will not prize
All the glory that he rides in,
When he gazes in my face;
He will say, ' O Love, thine eyes
Build the shrine my soul abides in;
And I kneel here for thy grace.'

" Then, ay, then he shall kneel low,
With the red-roan steed a-near him,
Which shall seem to understand—
Till I answer, ' Rise, and go!'
For the world must love and fear him
Whom I gift with heart and hand.

" Then he will arise so pale,
I shall feel my own lips tremble
With a *yes* I must not say—

Nathless maiden-brave, ' Farewell,'
I will utter and dissemble—
' Light to-morrow with today.'

" Then he'll ride among the hills
To the wide world past the river,
There to put away all wrong,
To make straight distorted wills,
And to empty the broad quiver
Which the wicked bear along.

" Three times shall a young foot-page
Swim the stream and climb the mountain,
And kneel down beside my feet—
' Lo! my master sends this gage,
Lady, for thy pity's counting!
What wilt thou exchange for it?'

" And the first time I will send
A white rosebud for a guerdon,
And the second time a glove;
But the third time—I may bend
From my pride, and answer—' Pardon,
If he comes to take my love.'

" Then the young foot-page will run—
Then my lover will ride faster,
Till he kneeleth at my knee:
' I am a duke's eldest son!
Thousand serfs do call me master,
But, O Love, I love but *thee!*'

" He will kiss me on the mouth
Then; and lead me as a lover,
Through the crowds that praise his deeds;
And, when soul-tied by one troth,
Unto him I will discover
That swan's nest among the reeds."

Little Ellie with her smile
Not yet ended, rose up gayly,
Tied the bonnet, donned the shoe—
And went homeward, round a mile,
Just to see, as she did daily,
What more eggs were with the *two*.

Pushing through the elm-tree copse
Winding by the stream, light-hearted,
Where the osier pathway leads,
Past the boughs she stoops, and stops.
Lo, the wild swan had deserted—
And a rat had gnawed the reeds!

Ellie went home sad and slow.
If she found the lover ever,
With his red-roan steed of steeds,
Sooth, I know not! but I know
She could never show him—never,
That swan's nest among the reeds.

ELIZABETH BARRETT BROWNING.

SEE WHAT A LOVELY SHELL

SEE what a lovely shell,
    Small and pure as a pearl,
Lying close to my foot,
Frail, but a work divine,
Made so fairily well
With delicate spire and whorl,
How exquisitely minute,
A miracle of design!

What is it? A learned man
Could give a clumsy name.
Let him name it who can,
The beauty would be the same.

The tiny cell is forlorn,
Void of the little living will
That made it stir on the shore.
Did he stand at the diamond door
Of his house in a rainbow frill?
Did he push, when he was uncurl'd,
A golden foot or a fairy horn
Thro' his dim water world?

Slight, to be crushed with a tap
Of my finger-nail on the sand,
Small, but a work divine,
Frail, but of force to withstand
Year upon year the shock
Of cataract seas that snap
The three-decker's oaken spine
Athwart the ledges of rock,
Here on the Breton strand!

TENNYSON.

THE ARROW AND THE SONG

I SHOT an arrow into the air,
It fell to earth, I knew not where;
For, so swiftly it flew, the sight
Could not follow it in its flight.

I breathed a song into the air,
It fell to earth, I knew not where;
For who has sight so keen and strong,
That it can follow the flight of song?

Long, long afterward in an oak
I found the arrow, still unbroke;
And the song, from beginning to end,
I found again in the heart of a friend.

LONGFELLOW.

THE BALLAD OF THE BOAT

THE stream was smooth as glass; we said, " Arise, and
let's away! "
The Siren sang beside the boat that in the rushes lay;
And spread the sail, and strong the oar; we gayly took
our way.
When shall the sandy bar be crossed? When shall we
find the bay?
The broadening flood swells slowly out o'er cattle-dotted
plains,
The stream is strong and turbulent, and dark with heavy
rains;
The laborer looks up to see our shallop speed away.
When shall the sandy bar be crossed? When shall we
find the bay?

Now are the clouds like fiery shrouds; the sun superbl
large,
Slow as an oak to woodman's stroke sinks flaming at the
marge.
The waves are bright with mirrored light as jacinths on
our way.
When shall the sandy bar be crossed? When shall we
find the bay?

The moon is high up in the sky, and now no more we see
The spreading river's either bank, and surging distantly
There booms a sudden thunder as of breakers far away.
Now shall the sandy bar be crossed, now shall we find the
    bay!
The seagull shrieks high overhead, and dimly to our sight
The moonlit crests of foaming waves gleam towering
    through the night.
We'll steal upon the mermaid soon, and start her from
    her lay,
When once the sandy bar is crossed, and we are in the bay.

What rises white and awful as a shroud-enfolded ghost?
What roar of rampant tumult bursts in clangor on the
    coast?
Pull back! pull back!   The raging flood sweeps every
    oar away.
O stream, is this thy bar of sand?   O boat is this thy bay?

RICHARD GARNETT.

THE BATTLE OF BLENHEIM

IT was a summer's evening,
   Old Kasper's work was done,
And he before his cottage door
   Was sitting in the sun;
And by him sported on the green
His little grandchild Wilhelmine.

She saw her brother Peterkin
   Roll something large and round,
Which he, beside the rivulet,
   In playing there had found.
He came to ask what he had found.
That was so large, and smooth, and round.

Old Kasper took it from the boy,
   Who stood expectant by;
And then the old man shook his head,
   And, with a natural sigh,
" 'Tis some poor fellow's skull," said he,
" Who fell in the great victory!

" I find them in the garden,
   For there's many here about;
And often when I go to plow,
   The plowshare turns them out;
For many thousand men," said he,
" Were slain in that great victory! "

" Now, tell us what 'twas all about,"
  Young Peterkin he cries;
And little Wilhelmine looks up
  With wonder-waiting eyes;
" Now tell us all about the war,
And what they killed each other for."

" It was the English," Kasper cried,
  " Who put the French to rout;
But what they killed each other for
  I could not well make out.
But everybody said," quoth he,
" That 'twas a famous victory!

" My father lived at Blenheim then,
  Yon little stream near-by:
They burned his dwelling to the ground,
  And he was forced to fly;
So with his wife and child he fled,
Nor had he where to rest his head.

" With fire and sword the country round
  Was wasted far and wide;
And many a childing mother then
  And new-born baby died.
But things like that, you know, must be
At every famous victory.

" They say it was a shocking sight
  After the field was won;
For many thousand bodies here
  Lay rotting in the sun.

But things like that, you know, must be
After a famous victory.

" Great praise the Duke of Marlborough won,
   And our good Prince Eugene."—
" Why, 'twas a very wicked thing! "
   Said. little Wilhelmine.
" Nay, nay, my little girl," quoth he,
" It was a famous victory!

" And everybody praised the Duke
   Who this great fight did win."—
" But what good came of it at last? "
   Quoth little Peterkin.
" Why, that I cannot tell," said he,
" But 'twas a famous victory! "

ROBERT SOUTHEY.

THE DAY IS DONE

THE day is done and the darkness
    Falls from the wings of Night,
As a feather is wafted downward
    From an eagle in its flight.

I see the lights of the village
    Gleam through the rain and the mist,
And a feeling of sadness comes o'er me
    That my soul cannot resist:

A feeling of sadness and longing,
    That is not akin to pain,
And resembles sorrow only
    As the mist resembles the rain.

Come, read to me some poem,
    Some simple and heartfelt lay,
That shall soothe this restless feeling,
    And banish the thoughts of day.

Not from the grand old masters,
    Not from the bards sublime,
Whose distant footsteps echo
    Through the corridors of Time.

For, like strains of martial music,
  Their mighty thoughts suggest
Life's endless toil and endeavor;
  And to-night I long for rest.

Read from some humbler poet,
  Whose songs gushed from his heart,
As showers from the clouds of summer,
  Or tears from the eyelids start;

Who, through long days of labor,
  And nights devoid of ease,
Still heard in his soul the music
  Of wonderful melodies.

Such songs have power to quiet
  The restless pulse of care,
And come like the benediction
  That follows after prayer.

Then read from the treasured volume
  The poem of thy choice,
And lend to the rhyme of the poet
  The beauty of thy voice.

And the night shall be filled with music,
  And the cares, that infest the day,
Shall fold their tents, like the Arabs,
  And as silently steal away.

                              LONGFELLOW.

THE GLADNESS OF NATURE

IS this a time to be cloudy and sad,
    When our mother Nature laughs around,
When even the deep blue heavens look glad,
    And gladness breathes from the blossoming ground?

There are notes of joy from the hang-bird and wren,
    And the gossip of swallows through all the sky;
The ground squirrel gladly chirps by his den,
    And the willing bee hums merrily by.

The clouds are at play in the azure space,
    And their shadows at play on the bright green vale;
And here they stretch to the frolic chase,
    And there they roll on the easy gale.

There's a dance of leaves in that aspen bower,
    There's a titter of wind in that beechen tree,
There's a smile on the fruit, and a smile on the flower,
    And a laugh from the brook that runs to the sea.

And look at the broad-faced sun, how he smiles
    On the dewey earth that smiles in his ray,
On the leaping waters and gay young isles,—
    Ay, look, and he'll smile thy gloom away.

                                    WILLIAM CULLEN BRYANT.

THE HOUSEKEEPER

THE frugal snail, with forecast of repose,
    Carries his house with him where'er he goes;
Peeps out,—and if there comes a shower of rain,
Retreats to his small domicile again.
Touch but a tip of him, a horn,—'tis well,—
He curls up in his sanctuary shell.
He's his own landlord, his own tenant; stay
Long as he will, he dreads no Quarter Day.
Himself he boards and lodges; both invites
And feasts himself; sleeps with himself over nights.
He spares the upholsterer trouble to procure
Chattels; himself is his own furniture,
And his sole riches. Wheresoe'er he roams,—
Knock when you will,—he's sure to be at home.

CHARLES LAMB.

THE LANDING OF THE PILGRIM
FATHERS IN NEW ENGLAND

THE breaking waves dashed high
On a stern and rock-bound coast,
And the woods against a stormy sky
Their giant branches tossed;

And the heavy night hung dark
The hills and waters o'er,
When a band of exiles moored their bark
On the wild New England shore.

Not as the conqueror comes,
They, the true-hearted, came;
Not with the roll of the stirring drums,
And the trumpet that sings of fame;

Not as the flying come,
In silence and in fear;—
They shook the depths of the desert gloom
With their hymns of lofty cheer.

Amidst the storm they sang,
And the stars heard and the sea;
And the sounding aisles of the dim woods rang
To the anthem of the free.

The ocean eagle soared
From his nest by the white wave's foam,
And the rocking pines of the forest roared—
This was their welcome home.

There were men with hoary hair
Amidst that pilgrim band;
Why had they come to wither there,
Away from their childhood's land?

There was woman's fearless eye,
Lit by her deep love's truth;
There was manhood's brow serenely high,
And the fiery heart of youth.

What sought they thus afar?
Bright jewels of the mine?
The wealth of seas, the spoils of war?—
They sought a faith's pure shrine!

Ay, call it holy ground,
The soil where first they trod;
They have left unstained what first they found,—
Freedom to worship God.

FELICIA D. HEMANS.

THE PET LAMB

THE dew was falling fast, the stars began to blink;
   I heard a voice, it said, " Drink, pretty creature,
      drink! "
And looking o'er the hedge, before me I espied
A snow-white mountain lamb with a maiden at its side.

No other sheep were near, the lamb was all alone,
And by a slender cord was tethered to a stone;
With one knee on the grass did the little maiden kneel,
While to that mountain lamb she gave its evening meal.

The lamb, while from her hand he thus his supper took,
Seemed to feast with head and ears, and his tail with
      pleasure shook.
" Drink, pretty creature, drink," she said, in such a tone
That I almost received her heart into my own.

'Twas little Barbara Lewthwaite, a child of beauty rare!
I watched them with delight; they were a lovely pair.
Now with her empty can the maiden turned away,
But ere ten yards were gone her footsteps did she stay.

Toward the lamb she looked; and from that shady place
I, unobserved, could see the workings of her face;
If Nature to her tongue could measured numbers bring,
Thus, thought I, to her lamb that little maid could sing:

" What ails thee, young one? What? Why pull so at
        thy cord?
Is it not well with thee—well both for bed and board?
Thy plot of grass is soft, and green as grass can be;
Rest, little young one, rest; what is't that aileth thee?

"What is it thou wouldst seek? What is wanting to thy
        heart?
Thy limbs, are they not strong? And beautiful thou art.
This grass is tender grass; these flowers they have no
        peers;
And that green corn, all day, is rustling in thy ears!

"If the sun be shining hot, do but stretch thy woolen
        chain;
This beech is standing by, its covert thou canst gain;
For rain and mountain storms! the like thou need'st not
        fear—
For rain and storm are things which scarcely can come
        here.

" Rest, little young one, rest; thou hast forgot the day
When my father found thee first in places far away;
Many flocks were on the hills, but thou wert owned by
        none,
And thy mother from thy side forever more was gone.

" He took thee in his arms and in pity brought thee home:
A blessed day for thee! then whither wouldst thou roam?
A faithful nurse thou hast; the dam that did thee yean
Upon the mountain tops no kinder could have been.

" Thou knowest that twice a day I have brought thee in
          this can
Fresh water from the brook, as clear as ever ran;
And twice in the day, when the ground is wet with dew,
I bring thee draughts of milk, warm milk it is, and new.

"Thy limbs will shortly be twice as stout as they are now,
Then I'll yoke thee to my cart, like a pony in the plow;
My playmate thou shalt be; and when the wind is cold
Our hearth shall be thy bed, our house shall be thy fold.

" It will not, will not rest! Poor creature, can it be
That 'tis thy mother's heart which is working so in thee?
Things that I know not of belike to thee are dear,
And dreams of things which thou canst neither see nor
          hear.

" Alas the mountain tops that look so green and fair!
I've heard of fearful winds and darkness that come there;
The little brooks that seem all pastime and all play,
When they are angry, roar like lions for their prey.

" Here thou need'st not dread the raven in the sky;
Night and day thou art safe,—our cottage is hard by.
Why bleat so after me? Why pull so at thy chain?
Sleep—and at break of day I will come to thee again! "

As homeward through the lane I went with lazy feet,
This song to myself did I oftentimes repeat;
And it seemed as I retraced the ballad, line by line,
That but half of it was hers, and one-half of it was mine.

Again, and once again, did I repeat the song;
" Nay," said I, " more than half to the damsel must
      belong,
For she looked with such a look, and she spake with such
      a tone,
That I almost received her heart into my own."

WORDSWORTH.

THE PLANTING OF THE APPLE TREE

COME, let us plant the apple tree.
   Cleave the tough greensward with the spade;
Wide let its hollow bed be made;
There gently lay the roots, and there
Sift the dark mould with kindly care,
And press it o'er them tenderly,
As round the sleeping infant's feet
We softly fold the cradle sheet;
So plant we the apple tree.

What plant we in the apple tree?
Buds, which the breath of summer days
Shall lengthen into leafy sprays;
Boughs where the thrush, with crimson breast,
Shall haunt, and sing and hide her nest;
We plant, upon the sunny lea,
A shadow for the noontide hour,
A shelter from the summer shower,
When we plant the apple tree.

What plant we in this apple tree?
Sweets for a hundred flowery springs
To load the May wind's restless wings,
When from the orchard row he pours
Its fragrance through our open doors;

A world of blossoms for the bee,
Flowers for the sick girl's silent room,
For the glad infant sprigs of bloom,
We plant with the apple tree.

What plant we in this apple tree?
Fruits that shall swell in sunny June,
And redden in the August noon,
And drop, when gentle airs come by,
That fan the blue September sky,
While children come with cries of glee,
And seek them where the fragrant grass
Betrays their bed to those who pass,
At the foot of the apple tree.

And when, above this apple tree,
The winter stars are quivering bright,
And winds go howling through the night,
Girls whose young eyes o'erflow with mirth,
Shall peel its fruit by cottage hearth,
And guests in prouder homes shall see,
Heaped with the grape of Cintra's vine
And golden orange of the Line,
The fruit of the apple tree.

The fruitage of this apple tree
Winds and our flag of stripe and star
Shall bear to coasts that lie afar,
Where men shall wonder at the view,
And ask in what fair groves they grew;

And sojourners beyond the sea
Shall think of childhood's careless day
And long, long hours of summer play,
In the shade of the apple tree.

Each year shall give this apple tree
A broader flush of roseate bloom,
A deeper maze of verduous gloom,
And loosen when the frost clouds lower,
The crisp brown leaves in thicker shower.
The years shall come and pass, but we
Shall hear no longer, where we lie,
The summer's songs, the autumn's sigh,
In the boughs of the apple tree.

And time shall waste this apple tree.
O, when its aged branches throw
Thin shadows on the ground below,
Shall fraud and force and iron will
Oppress the weak and helpless still?
What shall the tasks of mercy be,
Amid the toils, the strifes, the tears
Of those who live when length of years
Is wasting this apple tree?

"Who planted this old apple tree?"
The children of that distant day
Thus to some aged man shall say;
And, gazing on its mossy stem,
The gray-haired man shall answer them:

" A poet of the land was he,
Born in the rude but good old times;
'Tis said he made some quaint old rhymes
On planting the apple tree."

WILLIAM CULLEN BRYANT.

THE THREE FISHERS

THREE fishers went sailing out into the west,—
  Out into the west as the sun went down;
Each thought on the woman who loved him the best,
And the children stood watching them out of the town;
For men must work and women must weep,
And there's little to earn and many to keep,
Though the harbor bar be moaning.

Three wives sat up in the lighthouse tower,
And they trimmed the lamps as the sun went down;
They looked at the squall, and they looked at the shower,
And the night-rack came rolling up, ragged and brown.
But men must work and women must weep,
Though storms be sudden, and waters deep,
And the harbor be moaning.

Three corpses lay out on the shining sands
In the morning gleam as the tide went down,
And the women are weeping and wringing their hands,
For those who will never come home to the town;
For men must work and women must weep,—
And the sooner 'tis over, the sooner to sleep,
And good-by to the bar and its moaning.

CHARLES KINGSLEY.

THE WRECK OF THE HESPERUS

IT was the schooner *Hesperus,*
  That sailed the wintry sea;
And the skipper had taken his little daughter,
  To bear him company.

Blue were her eyes as the fairy-flax,
  Her cheeks like the dawn of day,
And her bosom white as the hawthorn buds,
  That ope in the month of May.

The skipper he stood beside the helm,
  His pipe was in his mouth,
And he watched how the veering flaw did blow
  The smoke now West, now South.

Then up and spake an old sailòr,
  Had sailed to the Spanish Main,
" I pray thee, put into yonder port,
  For I fear a hurricane.

" Last night the moon had a golden ring,
  And to-night no moon we see! "
The skipper, he blew a whiff from his pipe,
  And a scornful laugh laughed he.

Colder and louder blew the wind,
  A gale from the Northeast,
The snow fell hissing in the brine,
  And the billows frothed like yeast.

Down came the storm, and smote amain
  The vessel in its strength;
She shuddered and paused, like a frighted steed,
  Then leaped her cable's length.

" Come hither! come hither! my little daughtèr,
  And do not tremble so;
For I can weather the roughest gale
  That ever wind did blow."

He wrapped her warm in his seaman's coat
  Against the stinging blast;
He cut a rope from a broken spar,
  And bound her to the mast.

" O father! I hear the church bells ring,
  Oh say, what may it be? "
" 'Tis a fog-bell on a rock-bound coast! "
  And he steered for the open sea.

" O father! I hear the sound of guns,
  Oh say, what may it be? "
" Some ship in distress, that cannot live
  In such an angry sea! "

" O father! I see a gleaming light,
  Oh say, what may it be? "
But the father answered never a word,
  A frozen corpse was he.

Lashed to the helm, all stiff and stark,
  With his face turned to the skies,
The lantern gleamed through the gleaming snow
  On his fixed and glassy eyes.

Then the maiden clasped her hands and prayed
  That savèd she might be;
And she thought of Christ, who stilled the wave,
  On the Lake of Galilee.

And fast through the midnight dark and drear,
  Through the whistling sleet and snow,
Like a sheeted ghost, the vessel swept
  Toward the reef of Norman's Woe.

And ever the fitful gusts between
  A sound came from the land;
It was the sound of the trampling surf
  On the rocks and the hard sea-sand.

The breakers were right beneath her bows,
  She drifted a dreary wreck,
And a whooping billow swept the crew
  Like icicles from her deck.

She struck where the white and fleecy waves
  Looked soft as carded wool,
But the cruel rocks, they gored her side,
  Like the horns of an angry bull.

Her rattling shrouds, all sheathed in ice,
  With the mast went by the board;
Like a vessel of glass, she stove and sank,
  Ho! ho! the breakers roared!

At daybreak, on the bleak sea-beach,
  A fisherman stood aghast,
To see the form of a maiden fair,
  Lashed close to a drifting mast.

The salt sea was frozen on her breast,
  The salt tears in her eyes;
And he saw her hair, like the brown sea-weed,
  On the billows fall and rise.

Such was the wreck of the *Hesperus,*
  In the midnight and the snow!
Christ save us all from a death like this,
  On the reef of Norman's Woe!

                                        LONGFELLOW.

THE YELLOW VIOLET

WHEN beechen buds begin to swell,
    And woods the bluebird's warble know,
The yellow violet's modest bell
    Peeps from the last year's leaves below.

Ere russet fields their green resume,
    Sweet flower, I love, in forest bare,
To meet thee, when thy faint perfume
    Alone is in the virgin air.

Of all her train, the hands of Spring
    First plant thee in the watery mould,
And I have seen thee blossoming
    Beside the snow-bank's edges cold.

Thy parent sun who bade thee view
    Pale skies, and chilling moisture sip,
Has bathed thee in his own bright hue,
    And streaked with jet thy glowing lip.

Yet slight thy form, and low thy seat,
    And earthward bent thy gentle eye,
Unapt the passing view to meet,
    When loftier flowers are flaunting nigh.

53

Oft, in the sunless April day,
   Thy early smile has stayed my walk;
But mid the gorgeous blooms of May,
   I passed thee on thy humble stalk.

So they, who climb to wealth, forget
   The friends in darker fortunes tried.
I copied them—but I regret
   That I should ape the ways of pride.

And when the genial hour
   Awakes the painted tribes of light,
I'll not o'erlook the modest flower
   That made the woods of April bright.

              WILLIAM CULLEN BRYANT.

TO-DAY

SO here hath been dawning
   Another blue day:
Think will thou let it
   Slip useless away.

Out of Eternity
   This new day is born;
Into Eternity,
   At night will return.

Behold it aforetime
   No eye ever did;
So soon it forever
   From all eyes is hid.

Here hath been dawning
   Another blue day;
Think wilt thou let it
   Slip useless away.

THOMAS CARLYLE.

TO THE DAISY

IN youth from rock to rock I went,
   From hill to hill in discontent
Of pleasure high and turbulent,
      Most pleased when most uneasy;
But now my own delights I make,—
My thirst at every rill can slake,
And gladly Nature's love partake,
      Of thee, sweet daisy!

Thee winter in the garland wears
That thinly decks his few gray hairs;
Spring parts the clouds with softest airs
      That she may sun thee;
Whole summer fields are thine by right;
And Autumn, melancholy Wight!
Doth in thy crimson head delight
      When rains are on thee.

In shoals and bands, a morrice train,
Thou greet'st the traveler in the lane;
Pleased at his greeting thee again;
      Yet nothing daunted,
Nor grieved if thou be set at naught:
And oft alone in nooks remote
We meet thee, like a pleasant thought,
      When such are wanted.

Be violets in their secret mews
The flowers the wanton zephyrs choose;
Proud be the rose, with rains and dews
    Her head impearling.
Thou liv'st with less ambitious aim,
Yet hast not gone without thy fame;
Thou art indeed by many a claim
    The poet's darling.

If to a rock from rains he fly,
Or, some bright day of April sky,
Imprisoned by hot sunshine, lie
    Near the green holly,
And wearily at length should fare;
He needs but look about, and there
Thou art!—a friend at hand, to scare
    His melancholy.

A hundred times by rock or bower,
Ere thus I have lain crouched an hour,
Have I derived from thy sweet power
    Some apprehension;
Some steady love; some brief delight;
Some memory that had taken flight;
Some chime of fancy wrong or right;
    Or stray invention.

If stately passions in me burn,
And one chance look to thee should turn,
I drink out of an humble urn
    A lowlier pleasure;

The homely sympathy that heeds
The common life, our nature breeds;
A wisdom fitted to the needs
    Of hearts at leisure.

Fresh-smitten by the morning ray,
When thou art up, alert and gay,
Then, cheerful flower! my spirits play
    With kindred gladness:
And when, at dusk, by dews opprest
Thou sink'st, the image of thy rest
Hath often eased my pensive breast
    Of careful sadness.

And all day long I number yet,
All seasons through, another debt,
Which I, wherever thou art met,
    To thee am owing;
An instinct call it, a blind sense;
A happy, genial influence,
Coming one knows not how, nor whence,
    Nor whither going.

Child of the year! that round dost run
Thy pleasant course,—when day's begun
As ready to salute the sun
    As lark or leveret,
Thy long-lost praise thou shalt regain;
Nor be less dear to future men
Than in old time;—thou not in vain
    Art Nature's favorite.

                    WORDSWORTH.

TO THE FRINGED GENTIAN

THOU blossom, bright with autumn dew,
   And colored with the heaven's own blue,
That openest when the quiet light
Succeeds the keen and frosty night;

Thou comest not when violets lean
O'er wandering brooks and springs unseen,
Or columbines, in purple dressed,
Nod o'er the ground bird's hidden nest.

Thou waitest late, and com'st alone,
When woods are bare and birds are flown,
And frosts and shortening days portend
The aged Year is near his end.

Then doth thy sweet and quiet eye
Look through its fringes to the sky,
Blue—blue—as if that sky let fall
A flower from its cerulean wall.

I would that thus, when I shall see
The hour of death draw near to me,
Hope, blossoming within my heart,
May look to heaven as I depart.

WILLIAM CULLEN BRYANT.

UNDER THE GREENWOOD TREE

[From *As You Like It*.]

UNDER the greenwood tree
   Who loves to lie with me,
And turn his merry note
Unto the sweet bird's throat,
Come hither, come hither, come hither:
Here shall he see no enemy,
But winter and rough weather.

Who doth ambition shun,
And loves to live i' the sun,
Seeking the food he eats,
And pleas'd with what he gets,
Come hither, come hither, come hither:
Here shall he see no enemy,
But winter and rough weather.

SHAKESPEARE.

WOODMAN, SPARE THAT TREE

WOODMAN, spare that tree!
  Touch not a single bough!
In youth it sheltered me,
  And I'll protect it now.
'Twas my forefather's hand
  That placed it near his cot;
There, woodman, let it stand,
  Thy axe shall harm it not!

That old familiar tree,
  Whose glory and renown
Are spread o'er land and sea—
  And wouldst thou hew it down?
Woodman, forbear thy stroke!
  Cut not its earth-bound ties;
Oh, spare that aged oak,
  Now towering to the skies!

When but an idle boy
  I sought its grateful shade;
In all their gushing joy
  Here, too, my sisters played.
My mother kissed me here;
  My father pressed my hand—
Forgive this foolish tear,
  But let that old oak stand!

61

My heart-strings round thee cling,
  Close as thy bark, old friend!
Here shall the wild-bird sing,
  And still thy branches bend,
Old tree! the storm still brave!
  And, woodman, leave the spot;
While I've a chance to save,
  Thy axe shall harm it not.

GEORGE P. MORRIS.

HOME, SWEET HOME

'MID pleasures and palaces though we may roam,
    Be it ever so humble, there's no place like home!
A charm from the sky seems to hallow us there,
Which, seek through the world, is ne'er met with else-
    where.
Home, home, sweet, sweet home!
There's no place like home! There's no place like home!

An exile from home, splendor dazzles in vain;
O, give me my lowly thatched cottage again!
The birds singing sweetly that came at my call,—
Give me them,—and the peace of mind, dearer than all.
Home, home, sweet, sweet home!
There's no place like home! There's no place like home!

How sweet 'tis to sit 'neath a fond father's smile,
And the cares of a mother to soothe and beguile!
Let others delight 'mid new pleasures to roam,
But give me, oh, give me, the pleasures of home!
Home, home, sweet, sweet home!
There's no place like home! There's no place like home!

To thee I'll return, overburdened with care;
The heart's dearest solace will smile on me there;
No more from that cottage again will I roam;
Be it ever so humble, there's no place like home!
Home, home, sweet, sweet home!
There's no place like home! There's no place like home!
JOHN HOWARD PAYNE.

LULLABY FOR TITANIA

[From *A Midsummer Night's Dream.*]

FIRST FAIRY

YOU spotted snakes with double tongue,
  Thorny hedgehogs, be not seen;
Newts and blind-worms, do no wrong,
  Come not near our fairy queen.

Chorus.

  Philomel, with melody,
    Sing in our sweet lullaby;
Lulla, lulla, lullaby; lulla, lulla, lullaby;
Never harm, nor spell, nor charm,
    Come our lovely lady nigh;
    So, good-night, with lullaby.

SECOND FAIRY

Weaving spiders, come not here;
  Hence, for long-legg'd spinners, hence!
Beetles black, approach not near;
  Worm nor snail, do no offence.

64

Chorus.

Philomel, with melody,
Sing in our sweet lullaby;
Lulla, lulla, lullaby; lulla, lulla, lullaby;
Never harm, nor spell, nor charm,
Come our lovely lady nigh;
So, good-night, with lullaby.

SHAKESPEARE.

THE BLUE JAY

O BLUE JAY up in the maple tree,
   Shaking your throat with such bursts of glee,
 How did you happen to be so blue?
Did you steal a bit of the lake for your crest,
And fasten blue violets into your nest?
   Tell me, I pray you,—tell me true!

Did you dip your wings in azure dye,
When April began to paint the sky,
   That was pale with the winter's stay?
Or were you hatched from the bluebell bright,
'Neath the warm, gold breast of a sunbeam light,
   By the river one blue spring day?

O Blue Jay up in the maple tree,
A-tossing your saucy head at me,
   With ne'er a word for my questioning,
Pray, cease for a moment your " ting-a-link,"
And hear when I tell you what I think,—
   You bonniest bit of the spring.

I think when the fairies made the flowers,
To grow in these mossy fields of ours,
   Periwinkles and violets rare,
There was left of the spring's own color, blue,
Plenty to fashion a flower whose hue
   Would be richer than all, and so fair.

So, putting their wits together, they
Made one great blossom so bright and gay,
   The lily beside it seemed blurred;
And then they said, "We will toss it in air;
So many blue blossoms grow everywhere,
   Let this pretty one be a bird!"

SUSAN HARTLEY SWEET.

SIXTH YEAR

THE FLAG GOES BY

Hats off!
Along the street there comes
A blare of bugles, a ruffle of drums,
A flash of color beneath the sky:
Hats off!
The flag is passing by!

Blue and crimson and white it shines,
Over the steel-tipped, ordered lines.
Hats off!
The colors before us fly;
But more than the flag is passing by.

Sea fights and land fights, grim and great,
Fought to make and to save the State:
Weary marches and sinking ships;
Cheers of victory on dying lips;

Days of plenty and years of peace;
March of a strong land's swift increase;
Equal justice, right and law,
Stately honor and reverend awe;

Sign of a nation, great and strong
To ward her people from foreign wrong:
Pride and glory and honor,—all
Live in the colors to stand or fall.

Hats off!
Along the street there comes
A blare of bugles, a ruffle of drums;
And loyal hearts are beating high:
Hats off!
The flag is passing by!

HENRY HOLCOMB BENNETT.

ABOU BEN ADEM

ABOU BEN ADEM (may his tribe increase!)
  Awoke one night from a deep dream of peace,
And saw within the moonlight in his room,
Making it rich and like a lily in bloom,
An angel writing in a book of gold:
Exceeding peace had made Ben Adem bold,
And to the presence in the room he said,
"What writest thou?"—The vision raised its head,
And, with a look made of all sweet accord,
Answered, "The names of those who love the Lord."
"And is mine one?" said Abou. "Nay, not so,"
Replied the angel. Abou spoke more low,
But cheerily still; and said, "I pray thee, then,
Write me as one that loves his fellow men."

The angel wrote and vanished. The next night
It came again with a great wakening light,
And showed the names whom love of God had blessed,
And, lo! Ben Adem's name led all the rest!

LEIGH HUNT.

THE COMING OF SPRING

THERE'S something in the air
　　That's new and sweet and rare—
A scent of summer things,
A whir as if of wings.

There's something, too, that's new
In the color of the blue
That's in the morning sky,
Before the sun is high.

And though on plain and hill
'Tis winter, winter still,
There's something seems to say
That winter's had its day.

And all this changing tint,
This whispering stir and hint
Of bud and bloom and wing,
Is the coming of the spring.

And to-morrow or today
The brooks will break away
From their icy, frozen sleep,
And run, and laugh, and leap.

74

And the next thing, in the woods,
The catkins in their hoods
Of fur and silk will stand,
A sturdy little band.

And the tassels soft and fine
Of the hazel will entwine,
And the elder branches show
Their buds against the snow.

So, silently but swift,
Above the wintry drift,
The long days gain and gain,
Until on hill and plain,—

Once more, and yet once more,
Returning as before,
We see the bloom of birth
Make young again the earth.

NORA PERRY.

BURIAL OF SIR JOHN MOORE

NOT a drum was heard, not a funeral note,
   As his corse to the rampart we hurried;
Not a soldier discharged his farewell shot
   O'er the grave where our hero we buried.

We buried him darkly, at dead of night,
   The sods with our bayonets turning;
By the struggling moonbeam's misty light,
   And the lantern dimly burning.

No useless coffin enclosed his breast,
   Nor in sheet or in shroud we wound him;
But he lay like a warrior taking his rest,
   With his martial cloak around him.

Few and short were the prayers we said,
   And we spoke not a word of sorrow;
But we steadfastly gazed on the face of the dead,
   And we bitterly thought of the morrow.

We thought as we hollowed his narrow bed,
   And smoothed down his lonely pillow,
That the foe and the stranger would tread o'er his head,
   And we far away on the billow!

Lightly they'll talk of the spirit that's gone,
   And o'er his cold ashes upbraid him;
But little he'll reck, if they let him sleep on
   In the grave where a Briton has laid him!

But half of our heavy task was done
   When the clock tolled the hour for retiring;
And we heard the distant and random gun
   That the foe was sullenly firing.

Slowly and sadly we laid him down,
   From the field of his fame fresh and gory!
We carved not a line, we raised not a stone,
   But we left him alone with his glory.
                         CHARLES WOLFE.

CHRISTMAS BELLS

[Written December 25, 1864.]

I HEARD the bells on Christmas Day
Their old, familiar carols play,
    And wild and sweet
    The words repeat
Of peace on earth, good will to men!

And thought how, as the day had come,
The belfries of all Christendom
    Had rolled along
    The unbroken song
Of peace on earth, good will to men!

Till ringing, singing on its way,
The world revolved from night to day,
    A voice, a chime,
    A chant sublime
Of peace on earth, good will to men!

Then from each black, accursed mouth
The cannon thundered in the South,
    And with the sound
    The carols drowned
Of peace on earth, good will to men!

It was as if an earthquake rent
The hearth-stones of a continent,
　　And made forlorn
　　The households born
Of peace on earth, good will to men!

And in despair I bowed my head;
" There is no peace on earth," I said;
　　" For hate is strong,
　　And mocks the song
Of peace on earth, good will to men! "

Then pealed the bells more loud and deep:
" God is not dead; nor doth he sleep!
　　The Wrong shall fail,
　　And Right prevail,
With peace on earth, good will to men! "

LONGFELLOW.

EXILE OF ERIN

THERE came to the beach a poor Exile of Erin,
 The dew on his thin robe was heavy and chill;
For his country he sighed, when at twilight repairing,
 To wander alone by the wind-beaten hill:
But the day-star attracted his eye's sad devotion,
For it rose o'er his own native isle of the ocean,
Where once in the fire of his youthful emotion,
 He sang the bold anthem of Erin go bragh.

Sad is thy fate! said the heart-broken stranger;
 The wild deer and wolf to a covert can flee,
But I have no refuge from famine and danger,
 A home and a country remain not to me.
Never again, in the green sunny bowers,
Where my forefathers lived, shall I spend the sweet
  hours,
Or cover my harp with the wild-woven flowers,
 And strike to the numbers of Erin go bragh!

Erin, my country! though sad and forsaken,
 In dreams I revisit thy sea-beaten shore;
But alas! in a far foreign land I awaken,
 And sigh for the friends who can meet me no more!
Oh, cruel fate! wilt thou never replace me
In the mansion of peace—where no perils can chase me?
Never again shall my brothers embrace me?
 They died to defend me or live to deplore!

Where is my cabin door, fast by the wild wood?
   Sisters and sire! did ye weep for its fall?
Where is the mother that looked on my childhood?
   And where is the bosom friend dearer than all?
Oh! my sad heart! long abandoned by pleasure,
Why did it dote on a fast fading treasure?
Tears, like the raindrop, may fall without measure,
   But rapture and beauty they cannot recall.

Yet all its sad recollections suppressing,
   One dying wish my lone bosom can draw;
Erin! an exile bequeathes thee his blessing!
   Land of my forefathers! Erin go bragh!
Buried and cold, when my heart stills her motion,
Green be thy field,—sweetest isle of the ocean!
And thy harp-striking bards sing aloud with devotion,—
   Erin mavournin—Erin go bragh!

THOMAS CAMPBELL.

FOR A' THAT AND A' THAT

IS there for honest poverty
   That hangs his head, and a' that?
The coward slave, we pass him by;
We dare be poor for a' that.
For a' that and a' that.
Our toils obscure, and a' that;
The rank is but the guinea's stamp,—
The man's the gowd for a' that.

What though on hamely fare we dine,
Wear hoddin' gray, and a' that;
Gie fools their silks, and knaves their wine,—
A man's a man for a' that.
For a' that and a' that.
Their tinsel show and a' that;
The honest man though e'er so poor,
Is king o' men for a' that.

Ye see yon birkie ca'd a lord,
Wha struts and stares and a' that,—
Though hundreds worship at his word,
He's but a coof for a' that;
For a' that and a' that,
His riband, star and a' that,
The man of independent mind,
He looks and laughs at a' that.

A prince can mak a belted knight,
A marquis, duke and a' that;
But an honest man's aboon his might,—
Gude faith he maunna fa' that!
For a' that and a' that
Their dignities and a' that;
The pith o' sense and pride o' worth,
Are higher rank than a' that.

Then let us pray that come it may,—
As come it will for a' that,—
That sense and worth o'er a' the earth,
May bear the gree, and a' that.
For a' that and a' that,—
It's comin' yet for a' that
That man to man, the warld o'er,
Shall brothers be for a' that!

ROBERT BURNS.

"HOW THEY BROUGHT THE GOOD NEWS FROM GHENT TO AIX"

I SPRANG to the stirrup, and Joris, and he;
  I galloped, Dirck galloped, we galloped all three;
" Good speed! " cried the watch, as the gate-bolts undrew;
" Speed! " echoed the wall to us galloping through;
Behind shut the postern, the lights sank to rest,
And into the midnight we galloped abreast.

Not a word to each other; we kept the great pace
Neck by neck, stride by stride, never changing our place;
I turned in my saddle and made its girths tight,
Then shortened each stirrup, and set the pique right,
Rebuckled the cheek strap, chained slacker the bit,
Nor galloped less steadily Roland a whit.

'Twas moonset at starting; but while we drew near
Lokeren, the cocks crew and twilight dawned clear;
At Boom, a great yellow star came out to see;
At Düffeld, 'twas morning as plain as could be;
And from Mecheln church steeple we heard half the
      chime,
So, Joris broke silence with, " Yet there is time! "

At Aershot, up leaped of a sudden the sun,
And against him the cattle stood black every one,

To stare through the mist at us galloping past,
And I saw my stout galloper Roland at last,
With resolute shoulders, each butting away
The haze, as some bluff river headland its spray:

And his low head and crest, just one sharp ear bent back
For my voice, and the other pricked out on his track;
And one eye's black intelligence,—ever that glance
O'er its white edge at me, his own master, askance!
And the thick heavy spume flakes, that aye and anon
His fierce lips shook upward in galloping on.

By Hasselt, Dirck groaned; and cried Joris, " Stay spur!
Your Roos galloped bravely, the fault's not in her,
We'll remember at Aix "—for one heard the quick
        wheeze
Of her chest, saw the stretched neck and staggering knees,
And sunk tail, and horrible heave of the flank,
As down on her haunches she shuddered and sank.

So, we were left galloping, Joris and I,
Past Looz and past Tongres, no cloud in the sky;
The broad sun above laughed a pitiless laugh,
'Neath our feet broke the brittle bright stubble like chaff;
Till over by Dalhem a dome-spire sprang white,
And " Gallop," gasped Joris, " for Aix is in sight."

" How they'll greet us! "—and all in a moment his roan
Rolled neck and croup over, lay dead as a stone;
And there was my Roland to bear the whole weight
Of the news which alone could save Aix from her fate,

With his nostrils like pits full of blood to the brim,
And with circles of red for his eye-sockets' rim.

Then I cast loose my buffcoat, each holster let fall,
Shook off both my jack-boots, let go belt and all,
Stood up in the stirrup, leaned, patted his ear,
Called my Roland his pet name, my horse without peer;
Clapped my hands, laughed and sang, any noise, bad or
    good,
Till at length into Aix Roland galloped and stood.

And all I remember is—friends flocking round
As I sat with his head 'twixt my knees on the ground;
And no voice but was praising this Roland of mine,
As I poured down his throat our last measure of wine,
Which (the burgesses voted by common consent)
Was no more than his due who brought good news from
    Ghent.

ROBERT BROWNING.

I REMEMBER, I REMEMBER

I REMEMBER, I remember
  The house where I was born,
The little window where the sun
  Came peeping in at morn.
He never came a wink too soon,
  Nor brought too long a day;
But now I often wish the night
  Had borne my breath away!

I remember, I remember
  The roses, red and white,
The violets and the lily-cups,
  Those flowers made of light!
The lilacs where the robin built,
  And where my brother set
The laburnum on his birthday,—
  The tree is living yet!

I remember, I remember
  Where I was used to swing,
And thought the air must rush as fresh
  To swallows on the wing;
My spirit flew in feathers then,
  That is so heavy now,
And summer pools could hardly cool
  The fever on my brow!

I REMEMBER, I REMEMBER

I remember, I remember
  The fir-trees dark and high;
I used to think their slender tops
  Were close against the sky.
It was a childish ignorance,
  But now 'tis little joy
To know I'm farther off from heaven
  Than when I was a boy.

THOMAS HOOD.

KING SOLOMON AND THE ANTS

OUT from Jerusalem
  The king rode with his great
 War chiefs and lords of state,
And Sheba's queen with them;

Comely, but black withal,
  To whom, perchance, belongs
  That wondrous Song of Songs,
Sensuous and mystical,

Whereto devout souls turn
  In fond, ecstatic dream,
  And through its earth-born theme
The Love of loves discern.

Proud in the Syrian sun,
  In gold and purple sheen,
  The dusky Ethiop queen
Smiles on King Solomon.

Wisest of men he knew
  The languages of all
  The creatures great and small
That trod the earth or flew.

Across an ant-hill led
  The king's path, and he heard
  Its small folk, and their word
He thus interpreted:

" Here comes the king men greet
  As wise and good and just,
  To crush us in the dust
Under his heedless feet."

The great king bowed his head,
  And saw the wide surprise
  Of the Queen of Sheba's eyes
As he told her what they said.

" O king! " she whispered sweet,
  " Too happy fate have they
  Who perisʰ in thy way
Beneath thy gracious feet!

" Thou of the God-lent crown,
  Shall these vile creatures dare
  Murmur against thee where
The knees of kings kneel down? "

" Nay," Solomon replied,
  " The wise and strong should seek
  The welfare of the weak."
And turned his horse aside.

His train, with quick alarm,
Curved with their leader round
The ant-hill's peopled mound,
And left it free from harm.

The jewelled head bent low;
" O king!" she said, " henceforth
The secret of thy worth
And wisdom well I know.

" Happy must be the State
Whose ruler heedeth more
The murmurs of the poor
Than flatteries of the great."

JOHN GREENLEAF WHITTIER.

LADY CLARE

IT was the time when lilies blow,
  And clouds are highest up in air,
Lord Ronald brought a lily-white doe
  To give his cousin, Lady Clare.

I trow they did not part in scorn:
  Lovers long betrothed were they:
They two will wed the morrow morn:
  God's blessings on the day!

" He does not love me for my birth,
  Nor for my lands so broad and fair;
He loves me for my own true worth,
  And that is well," said Lady Clare.

In there came old Alice the nurse,
  Said, " Who was this that went from thee?"
" It was my cousin," said Lady Clare,
  " To-morrow he weds with me."

" O God be thanked!" said Alice the nurse,
  " That all comes round so just and fair:
Lord Ronald is heir of all your lands,
  And you are not the Lady Clare."

" Are ye out of your mind, my nurse, my nurse? "
　　Said Lady Clare, " that ye speak so wild? "
" As God is above," said Alice the nurse,
　　" I speak the truth: you are my child.

" The old Earl's daughter died at my breast;
　　I speak the truth, as I live by bread!
I buried her like my own sweet child,
　　And put my child in her stead."

" Falsely, falsely have ye done,
　　O mother," she said, " if this be true,
To keep the best man under the sun
　　So many years from his due."

" Nay, now, my child," said Alice the nurse,
　　" But keep the secret for your life,
And all you have will be Lord Ronald's
　　When you are man and wife."

" If I'm a beggar born," she said,
　　" I will speak out, for I dare not lie.
Pull off, pull off the brooch of gold,
　　And fling the diamond necklace by."

" Nay, now, my child," said Alice the nurse,
　　" But keep the secret all ye can."
She said, " Not so: but I will know
　　If there be any faith in man."

" Nay now, what faith? " said Alice the nurse,
  " The man will cleave unto his right."
"And he shall have it," the lady replied,
  " Tho' I should die to-night."

" Yet give one kiss to your mother dear!
  Alas, my child, I sinned for thee."
" O mother, mother, mother," she said,
  " So strange it seems to me.

" Yet here's a kiss for my mother dear,
  My mother dear, if this be so,
And lay your hand upon my head,
  And bless me, mother, ere I go."

She clad herself in a russet gown,
  She was no longer Lady Clare:
She went by dale and she went by down,
  With a single rose in her hair.

The lily-white doe Lord Ronald had brought
  Leapt up from where she lay,
Dropt her head in the maiden's hand,
  And follow'd her all the way.

Down stept Lord Ronald from his tower:
  " O Lady Clare, you shame your worth!
Why come you drest like a village maid,
  That are the flower of the earth? "

" If I come drest like a village maid,
　I am but as my fortunes are:
I am a beggar born," she said,
　" And not the Lady Clare."

" Play me no tricks," said Lord Ronald,
　" For I am yours in word and deed.
Play me no tricks," said Lord Ronald,
　" Your riddle is hard to read."

Oh, and proudly stood she up!
　Her heart within her did not fail:
She look'd into Lord Ronald's eyes,
　And told him all her nurse's tale.

He laughed a laugh of merry scorn:
　He turned and kissed her where she stood:
" If you are not the heiress born,
　And I," said he, " the next in blood—

" If you are not the heiress born,
　And I," said he, " the lawful heir,
We two will wed to-morrow morn,
　And you shall still be Lady Clare."
　　　　　　　ALFRED TENNYSON.

MY HEART'S IN THE HIGHLANDS

MY heart's in the Highlands, my heart is not here;
My heart's in the Highlands a-chasing the deer;
Chasing the wild deer and following the roe,
My heart's in the Highlands wherever I go.
Farewell to the Highlands, farewell to the North,
The birthplace of valor, the country of worth;
Wherever I wander, wherever I rove,
The hills of the Highlands forever I love.

Farewell to the mountains high covered with snow;
Farewell to the straths and green valleys below;
Farewell to the forests and wild hanging woods;
Farewell to the torrents and loud pouring floods.
My heart's in the Highlands, my heart is not here,
My heart's in the Highlands a-chasing the deer;
Chasing the wild deer and following the roe,
My heart's in the Highlands wherever I go.

ROBERT BURNS.

ONE BY ONE

ONE by one the sands are flowing,
  One by one the moments fall;
Some are coming, some are going;
  Do not strive to grasp them all.

One by one thy duties wait thee—
  Let thy whole strength go to each,
Let no future dreams elate thee,
  Learn thou first what these can teach.

One by one (bright gifts from heaven)
  Joys are sent thee here below;
Take them readily when given—
  Ready, too, to let them go.

One by one thy griefs shall meet thee;
  Do not fear an arméd band;
One will fade as others greet thee—
  Shadows passing through the land.

Do not look at life's long sorrow;
  See how small each moment's pain;
God will help thee for to-morrow,
  So, each day, begin again.

Every hour that fleets so slowly
    Has its task to do or bear;
Luminous the crown, and holy,
    When each gem is set with care.

Do not linger with regretting,
    Or for passing hours despond;
Nor, thy daily toil forgetting,
    Look too eagerly beyond.

Hours are golden links, God's token,
    Reaching heaven; but, one by one,
Take them, lest the chain be broken
    Ere the pilgrimage be done.

ADELAIDE A. PROCTOR.

ORPHEUS WITH HIS LUTE

[From *Henry VIII*.]

ORPHEUS with his lute made trees,
  And the mountain tops that freeze,
 Bow themselves, when he did sing:
To his music, plants and flowers
Ever sprung; as sun and showers
  There had made a lasting spring.

Everything that heard him play,
Even the billows of the sea,
  Hung their heads and then lay by.
In sweet music is such art,
Killing care and grief of heart
  Fall asleep, or, hearing, die.

SHAKESPEARE.

QUIET WORK

ONE lesson, Nature, let me learn of thee,
   One lesson which in every wind is blown,
One lesson of two duties kept at one
Though the loud world proclaim their enmity—

Of toil unsevered from tranquillity;
Of labor, that in lasting fruit outgrows
Far noisier schemes, accomplished in repose,
Too great for haste, too high for rivalry.

Yes, while on earth a thousand discords ring,
Man's senseless uproar mingling with his toil,
Still do thy quiet ministers move on,

Their glorious tasks in silence perfecting;
Still working, blaming still our vain turmoil,
Laborers that shall not fail, when man is gone.
                                    MATTHEW ARNOLD.

REBECCA'S HYMN

WHEN Israel, of the Lord beloved,
  Out of the land of bondage came,
Her father's God before her moved,
  An awful guide in smoke and flame.
By day, along the astonish'd lands
  The cloudy pillar glided slow;
By night Arabia's crimson'd sands
  Returned the fiery column's glow.

There rose the choral hymn of praise,
  And trump and timbrel answered keen,
And Zion's daughters poured their lays,
  With priest's and warrior's voice between.
No portents now our foes amaze,
  Forsaken Israel wanders lone;
Our fathers would not know Thy ways,
  And Thou hast left them to their own.

But present still, though now unseen,
  When brightly shines the prosperous day,
Be thoughts of Thee a cloudy screen
  To temper the deceitful ray.
And oh, when stoops on Judah's path
  In shade and storm the frequent night,
Be Thou, long-suffering, slow to wrath,
  A burning and a shining light!

Our harps we left by Babel's streams,
 The tyrant's jest, the Gentile's scorn;
No censer round our altar beams,
 And mute our timbrel, harp, and horn.
But Thou hast said, " The blood of goat,
 The flesh of rams I will not prize;
A contrite heart, an humble thought,
 Are mine accepted sacrifice."

SIR WALTER SCOTT.

REST

R EST is not quitting
　　The busy career;
Rest is the fitting
　　Of self to one's sphere:

'Tis the brook's motion,
　　Clear without strife;
Fleeting to ocean,
　　After its life:

'Tis loving and serving
　　The highest and best;
'Tis onward, unswerving.
　　And this is true rest.

Goethe.

RUTH

SHE stood breast high amid the corn,
    Clasped by the golden light of morn,
Like the sweetheart of the sun,
Who many a glowing kiss had won.

On her cheek an autumn flush,
Deeply ripened;—such a blush
In the midst of brown was born,
Like red poppies grown with corn.

Round her eyes her tresses fell,
Which were blackest none could tell,
But long lashes veiled a light,
That had else been all too bright.

And her hat with shady brim,
Made her tressy forehead dim;—
Thus she stood amid the stooks,
Praising God with sweetest looks:—

Sure, I said, heav'n did not mean,
Where I reap thou shouldst but glean,
Lay thy sheaf adown and come,
Share my harvest and my home.

THOMAS HOOD.

THE BRIDGE

I STOOD on the bridge at midnight,
  As the clocks were striking the hour,
And the moon rose o'er the city,
  Behind the dark church tower.

I saw her bright reflection
  In the waters under me,
Like a golden goblet falling
  And sinking into the sea.

And far in the hazy distance
  Of that lovely night in June,
The blaze of the flaming furnace
  Gleamed redder than the moon.

Among the long black rafters
  The wavering shadows lay,
And the current that came from the ocean
  Seemed to lift and bear them away;

As, sweeping and eddying through them,
  Rose the belated tide,
And, streaming into the moonlight,
  The sea-weed floated wide.

And like those waters rushing
　　Among the wooden piers,
A flood of thoughts came o'er me
　　That filled my eyes with tears.

How often, oh, how often,
　　In the days that had gone by,
I had stood on that bridge at midnight
　　And gazed on that wave and sky!

How often, oh, how often,
　　I had wished that the ebbing tide
Would bear me away on its bosom
　　O'er the ocean wild and wide!

For my heart was hot and restless,
　　And my life was full of care,
And the burden laid upon me
　　Seemed greater than I could bear.

But now it has fallen from me,
　　It is buried in the sea;
And only the sorrow of others
　　Throws its shadow over me.

Yet whenever I cross the river
　　On its bridge with wooden piers,
Like the odor of brine from the ocean
　　Comes the thought of other years.

And I think how many thousands
　Of care encumbered men,
Each bearing his burden of sorrow,
　Have crossed the bridge since then.

I see the long procession
　Still passing to and fro,
The young heart hot and restless,
　And the old subdued and slow!

And forever and forever,
　As long as the river flows,
As long as the heart has passions,
　As long as life has woes;

The moon and its broken reflection
　And its shadows shall appear,
As the symbol of love in heaven,
　And its wavering image here.

LONGFELLOW.

THE BUILDERS

ALL are architects of Fate,
   Working in these walls of Time;
Some with massive deeds and great,
   Some with ornaments of rhyme.

Nothing useless is, or low;
   Each thing in its place is best;
And what seems but idle show
   Strengthens and supports the rest.

For the structure that we raise,
   Time is with materials filled;
Our todays and yesterdays
   Are the blocks with which we build.

Truly shape and fashion these;
   Leave no yawning gaps between;
Think not, because no man sees,
   Such things will remain unseen.

In the elder days of Art,
   Builders wrought with greatest care
Each minute and unseen part;
   For the Gods see everywhere.

Let us do our work as well,
  Both the unseen and the seen;
Make the house where Gods may dwell
  Beautiful, entire and clean.

Else our lives are incomplete,
  Standing in these walls of Time,
Broken stairways, where the feet
  Stumble, as they seek to climb.

Build today, then, strong and sure,
  With a firm and ample base;
And ascending and secure
  Shall to-morrow find its place.

Thus alone can we attain
  To those turrets, where the eye
Sees the world as one vast plain,
  And one boundless reach of sky.

LONGFELLOW.

THE DESTRUCTION OF SENNACHERIB

THE Assyrian came down like a wolf on the fold,
    And his cohorts were gleaming in purple and gold;
And the sheen of their spears was like stars on the sea,
When the blue waves rolled nightly on deep Galilee.

Like the leaves of the forest when summer is green,
That host with their banners at sunset were seen;
Like the leaves of the forest when autumn hath blown,
That host on the morrow lay withered and strown.

For the Angel of Death spread his wings on the blast,
And breathed in the face of the foe as he passed;
And the eyes of the sleepers waxed deadly and chill,
And their hearts but once heaved, and forever grew still!

And there lay the steed with his nostrils all wide,
But through it there rolled not the breath of his pride:
And the foam of his gasping lay white on the turf,
And cold as the spray of the rock-beating surf.

And there lay the rider, distorted and pale,
With the dew on his brow and the rust on his mail;
And the tents were all silent, the banners alone,
The lances unlifted, the trumpets unblown.

And the widows of Ashur are loud in their wail,
And the idols are broke in the temple of Baal;
And the might of the Gentile, unsmote by the sword,
Hath melted like snow in the glance of the Lord!

LORD BYRON.

THE DROVERS

THROUGH heat and cold, and shower, and sun,
    Still onward cheerly driving!
There's life alone in duty done,
    And rest alone in striving.
But see the day is closing cool,
    The woods are dim before us;
The white fog of the wayside pool
    Is creeping slowly o'er us.

The night is falling, comrades mine,
    Our footsore beasts are weary,
And through yon elms the tavern sign
    Looks out upon us cheery.
The landlord beckons from his door,
    His beechen fire is glowing;
These ample barns, with feed in store,
    Are filled to overflowing.

From many a valley frowned across
    By brows of rugged mountains;
From hillsides where, through spongy moss,
    Gush out the river fountains;
From quiet farm fields, green and low,
    And bright with blooming clover;
From vales of corn the wandering crow
    No richer hovers over;

Day after day our way has been,
　O'er many a hill and hollow;
By lake and stream, by wood and glen,
　Our stately drove we follow.
Through dust-clouds rising thick and dun,
　As smoke of battle o'er us,
Their white horns glisten in the sun,
　Like plumes and crests before us.

We see them slowly climb the hill,
　As slow behind it sinking;
Or, thronging close, from roadside rill,
　Or sunny lakelet, drinking.
Now crowding in the narrow road,
　In thick and struggling masses,
They glare upon the teamster's load,
　Or rattling coach that passes.

Anon, with toss of horn and tail,
　And paw of hoof, and bellow,
They leap some farmer's broken pale,
　O'er meadow close or fallow.
Forth comes the startled goodman; forth
　Wife, children, house-dog, sally
　'ill once more on their dusty path
　The baffled truants rally.

We drive no starvelings, scraggy grown,
　Loose-legged, and ribbed and bony,
Like those who grind their noses down
　On pastures bare and stony,—

Lank oxen, rough as Indian dogs,
    And cows too lean for shadows,
Disputing feebly with the frogs
    The crop of saw-grass meadows!

In our good drove, so sleek and fair,
    No bones of leanness rattle;
No tottering hide-bound ghosts are there,
    Or Pharaoh's evil cattle.
Each stately beeve bespeaks the hand
    That fed him unrepining;
The fatness of a goodly land
    In each dun hide is shining.

We've sought them where in warmest nooks,
    The freshest feed is growing,
By sweetest springs and clearest brooks
    Through honeysuckle flowing;
Wherever hillsides, sloping south,
    Are bright with early grasses,
Or, tracking green the lowland's drouth,
    The mountain streamlet passes.

But now the day is closing cool,
    The woods are dim before us,
The white fog of the wayside pool
    Is creeping slowly o'er us.
The cricket to the frog's bassoon
    His shrillest time is keeping;
The sickle of yon setting moon
    The meadow mist is reaping.

The night is falling, comrades mine,
　Our footsore beasts are weary,
And through yon elms the tavern sign
　Looks out upon us cheery.
To-morrow, eastward with our charge
　We'll go to meet the dawning,
Ere yet the pines of Kearsarge
　Have seen the sun of morning.

When snowflakes o'er the frozen earth,
　Instead of birds, are flitting;
When children throng the glowing hearth,
　And quiet wives are knitting;
While in the firelight strong and clear
　Young eyes of pleasure glisten,
To tales of all we see and hear
　The ears of home shall listen.

By many a northern lake and hill,
　From many a mountain pasture,
Shall Fancy play the drover still,
　And speed the long night faster.
Then let us on, through shower and sun,
　And heat and cold be driving,
There's life alone in duty done,
　And rest alone in striving.

JOHN GREENLEAF WHITTIER.

THE HURRICANE

L ORD of the winds! I feel thee nigh,
     I know thy breath in the burning sky!
And I wait with a thrill in every vein,
For the coming of the hurricane!

And lo! on the wing of the heavy gales,
Through the boundless arch of heaven he sails;
Silent and slow and terribly strong,
The mighty shadow is borne along,
Like the dark eternity to come;
While the world below, dismayed and dumb,
Through the calm of the thick hot atmosphere,
Looks up at its gloomy folds with fear.

They darken fast; and the golden blaze
Of the sun is quenched in the lurid haze,
And he sends through the shade a funeral ray⌐
A glare that is neither night nor day,
A beam that touches, with hues of death,
The clouds above and the earth beneath.
To its covert glides the silent bird,
While the hurricane's distant voice is heard
Uplifted among the mountains round,
And the forests hear and answer the sound.

He is come! he is come! do ye not behold
His ample robes on the winds unrolled?
Giant of air we bid thee hail!—
How his gray skirts toss in the whirling gale;
How his huge and writhing arms are bent
To clasp the zone of the firmament,
And fold at length, in their dark embrace,
From mountain to mountain the visible space.

Darker—still darker! the whirlwinds bear
The dust of the plains to the middle air;
And hark to the crashing, long and loud,
Of the chariot of God in the thundercloud!
You may trace its path by the flashes that start
From the rapid wheels where'er they dart,
As the fire-bolts leap to the world below,
And flood the skies with a lurid glow.

What roar is that? 'tis the rain that breaks
In torrents away from the airy lakes,
Heavily poured on the shuddering ground,
And shedding a nameless horror round.
Ah! well-known woods, and mountains, and skies,
With the very clouds! ye are lost to my eyes.
I seek ye vainly, and see in your place
The shadowy tempest that sweeps through space,
A whirling ocean that fills the wall
Of the crystal heaven, and buries all.
And I, cut off from the world, remain
Alone with the terrible hurricane.

WILLIAM CULLEN BRYANT.

THE HERITAGE

THE rich man's son inherits lands,
   And piles of brick, and stone, and gold,
And he inherits soft white hands,
   And tender flesh that fears the cold,
   Nor dares to wear a garment old;
A heritage, it seems to me,
One scarce would wish to hold in fee.

The rich man's son inherits cares;
   The bank may break, the factory burn,
A breath may burst his bubble shares,
   And soft white hands could hardly earn
   A living that would serve his turn;
A heritage, it seems to me,
One scarce would wish to hold in fee.

The rich man's son inherits wants,
   His stomach craves for dainty fare;
With sated heart he hears the pants
   Of toiling hinds with brown arms bare,
   And wearies in his easy-chair;
A heritage, it seems to me,
One scarce would wish to hold in fee.

What doth the poor man's son inherit?
  Stout muscles and a sinewy heart,
A hardy frame, a hardier spirit;
  King of two hands, he does his part
  In every useful toil and art;
A heritage, it seems to me,
A king might wish to hold in fee.

What doth the poor man's son inherit?
  Wishes o'erjoyed with humble things,
A rank adjudged by toil-won merit,
  Content that from employment springs,
  A heart that in his labor sings;
A heritage, it seems to me,
A king might wish to hold in fee.

What doth the poor man's son inherit?
  A patience learned of being poor,
Courage, if sorrow come, to bear it,
  A fellow-feeling that is sure
  To make the outcast bless his door;
A heritage, it seems to me,
A king might wish to hold in fee.

O rich man's son! there is a toil
  That with all others level stands;
Large charity doth never soil,
  But only whiten, soft white hands,—
  This is the best crop from thy lands;
A heritage, it seems to me,
Worth being rich to hold in fee.

O poor man's son! scorn not thy state;
　There is worse weariness than thine
In merely being rich and great;
　Toil only gives the soul to shine,
　And makes rest fragrant and benign;
A heritage, it seems to me,
Worth being poor to hold in fee.

Both, heirs to some six feet of sod,
　Are equal in the earth at last;
Both, children of the same dear God,
　Prove title to your heirship vast
　By record of a well-filled past;
A heritage, it seems to me,
Well worth a life to hold in fee.

JAMES RUSSELL LOWELL

THE MARSEILLAISE

YE sons of Freedom, wake to glory!
  Hark! Hark! what myriads bid you rise—
Your children, wives, and grandsires hoary,
  Behold their tears and hear their cries!
Shall hateful tyrants, mischiefs breeding,
  With hireling hosts, a ruffian band,
  Affright and desolate the land,
While peace and liberty lie bleeding?
  To arms! to arms! ye brave!
  The avenging sword unsheathe;
March on! march on! all hearts resolved
  On victory or death.

Now, now, the dangerous storm is rolling,
  Which treacherous kings confederate raise;
The dogs of war, let loose, are howling,
  And lo! our fields and cities blaze;
And shall we basely view the ruin,
  While lawless force, with guilty stride,
  Spreads desolation far and wide,
With crimes and blood their hands imbruing?
  To arms! to arms! ye brave,
  The avenging sword unsheathe;
March on! march on! all hearts resolved
  On victory or death.

With luxury and pride surrounded,
   The vile, insatiate despots dare,—
Their thirst of power and gold unbounded,—
   To mete and vend the light and air,
Like beasts of burden would they load us,
   Like gods would bid their slaves adore;
   But man is man and who is more?
Then shall they longer lash and goad us?
   To arms! to arms! ye brave,
   The avenging sword unsheathe;
March on! march on! all hearts resolved
   On victory or death.

O Liberty! can man resign thee,
   Once having felt thy generous flame?
Can dungeons, bolts, or bars confine thee,
   Or whip thy noble spirit tame?
Too long the world has wept bewailing
   That Falsehood's dagger tyrants wield;
   But Freedom is our sword and shield,
And all their arts are unavailing.
   To arms! to arms! ye brave,
   The avenging sword unsheathe;
March on! march on! all hearts resolved
   On victory or death.

                    ROUGET DE L'ISLE.

THE MINSTREL BOY

THE minstrel boy to the war is gone,
  In the ranks of death you'll find him;
His father's sword he has girded on,
  And his wild harp slung behind him.—
" Land of song! " said the warrior bard,
  " Though all the world betrays thee,
" One sword, at least, thy rights shall guard,
  " One faithful harp shall praise thee! "

The minstrel fell!—but the foeman's chain
  Could not bring his proud soul under;
The harp he loved ne'er spoke again,
  For he tore its chords asunder,
And said, " No chains shall sully thee,
  " Thou soul of love and bravery!
" Thy songs were made for the pure and free,
  " They shall never sound in slavery! "

THOMAS MOORE.

THE NECKAN

IN summer on the headlands,
  The Baltic Sea along,
Sits Neckan with his harp of gold,
  And sings his plaintive song.

Green rolls beneath the headlands,
  Green rolls the Baltic Sea;
And there, below the Neckan's feet,
  His wife and children be.

He sings not of the ocean,
  Its shells and roses pale;
Of earth, of earth, the Neckan sings,
  He hath no other tale.

He sits upon the headlands,
  And sings a mournful stave
Of all he saw and felt on earth,
  Far from the kind sea-wave.

Sings how, a knight, he wandered
  By castle, field, and town—
But earthly knights have harder hearts
  Than the sea-children own.

Sings of his earthly bridal—
  Priests, knights and ladies gay.
"—And who art thou," the priest began,
  " Sir Knight, who wedd'st today? "

" I am no knight," he answered;
  " From the sea waves I come."
The knights drew sword, the ladies screamed,
  The surpliced priest stood dumb.

He sings how from the chapel
  He vanished with his bride,
And bore her down to the sea halls,
  Beneath the salt sea tide.

He sings how she sits weeping
  'Mid shells that round her lie.
" False Neckan shares my bed," she weeps;
  " No Christian mate have I."

He sings how through the billows
  He rose to earth again,
And sought a priest to sign the cross,
  That Neckan Heaven might gain.

He sings how, on an evening,
  Beneath the birch tree cool,
He sate and played his harp of gold,
  Beside the river pool.

Beside the pool sate Neckan—
    Tears filled his mild blue eye.
On his white mule, across the bridge,
    A cassocked priest rode by.

" Why sittest thou there, O Neckan,
    And play'st thy harp of gold?
Sooner shall this my staff bear leaves,
    Than thou shalt Heaven behold.—"

But lo! the staff is budded!
    It green'd, it branched, it waved.
" O ruth of God," the priest cried out,
    " This lost sea creature saved!"

The cassocked priest rode onwards,
    And vanished with his mule;
But Neckan in the twilight gray
    Wept by the river pool.

He wept: " The earth hath kindness,
    The sea, the starry poles;
Earth, sea, and sky, and God above—
    But ah, not human souls!"

In summer, on the headlands,
    The Baltic Sea along,
Sits Neckan with his harp of gold,
    And sings this plaintive song.

MATTHEW ARNOLD.

THE SONG OF THE SHIRT

WITH fingers weary and worn,
   With eyelids heavy and red,
A woman sat in unwomanly rags,
   Plying her needle and thread,—
Stitch! stitch! stitch!
   In poverty, hunger and dirt;
And still with a voice of dolorous pitch
   She sang the " Song of the Shirt! "

" Work! work! work!
   While the cock is crying aloof!
And work—work—work!
   Till the stars shine through the roof!
It's oh! to be a slave
   Along with the barbarous Turk,
Where woman has never a soul to save,
   If this is Christian work!

" Work—work—work!
   Till the brain begins to swim!
Work—work—work!
   Till the eyes are heavy and dim!
Seam, and gusset, and band,
   Band, and gusset, and seam,
Till over the buttons I fall asleep,
   And sew them on in a dream!

" O men, with sisters dear!
　O men, with mothers and wives!
It is not linen you're wearing out,
　But human creatures' lives!
Stitch—stitch—stitch!
　In poverty, hunger, and dirt,—
Sewing at once with a double thread,
　A shroud as well as a shirt!

" But why do I talk of death,—
　That phantom of grisly bone?
I hardly fear his terrible shape,
　It seems so like my own,—
　It seems so like my own,
Because of the fasts I keep;
　O God! that bread should be so dear,
And flesh and blood so cheap!

" Work! work! work!
　My labor never flags;
And what are its wages? A bed of straw,
　A crust of bread—and rags,
That shattered roof—and this naked floor—
　A table—a broken chair—
And a wall so blank, my shadow I thank
　For sometimes falling there!

" Work—work—work!
　From weary chime to chime!
Work—work—work!
　As prisoners work for crime!

Band, and gusset, and seam,
　　Seam, and gusset, and band,—
Till the heart is sick and the brain benumbed,
　　As well as the weary hand.

" Work—work—work!
　　In the dull December light!
And work—work—work!
　　When the weather is warm and bright!
While underneath the eaves
　　The brooding swallows cling,
As if to show me their sunny backs,
　　And twit me with the spring.

" Oh, but to breathe the breath
　　Of the cowslip and primrose sweet,—
With the sky above my head,
　　And the grass beneath my feet!
For only one short hour
　　To feel as I used to feel,
Before I knew the woes of want
　　And the walk that costs a meal!

' Oh, but for one short hour,—
　　A respite, however brief!
No blessed leisure for love or hope,
　　But only time for grief!
A little weeping would ease my heart;
　　But in their briny bed
My tears must stop, for every drop
　　Hinders needle and thread! "

With fingers weary and worn,
  With eyelids heavy and red,
A woman sat in unwomanly rags,
  Plying her needle and thread,—
Stitch! stitch! stitch!
  In poverty, hunger and dirt;
And still with a voice of dolorous pitch—
Would that its tone could reach the rich!—
  She sang the " Song of the Shirt! "

                              THOMAS HOOD.

THE SPACIOUS FIRMAMENT ON HIGH

THE spacious firmament on high,
With all the blue ethereal sky,
And spangled heavens, a shining frame,
Their great Original proclaim;
The unwearied sun, from day to day,
Does his Creator's power display,
And publishes to every land
The work of an Almighty hand.

Soon as the evening shades prevail,
The moon takes up the wondrous tale,
And nightly to the listening earth
Repeats the story of her birth;
While all the stars that round her burn,
And all the planets in their turn,
Confirm the tidings as they roll,
And spread the truth from pole to pole.

What though, in solemn silence, all
Move round the dark terrestrial ball?
What though no real voice or sound
Amid their radiant orbs be found?
In Reason's ear they all rejoice,
And utter forth a glorious voice,
Forever singing, as they shine,
"The Hand that made us is divine!"

JOSEPH ADDISON

THE WATCH ON THE RHINE

A VOICE resounds like thunder peal,
'Mid dashing waves and clang of steel,—
" The Rhine! the Rhine! the German Rhine!
Who guards today thy stream divine? "
Dear Fatherland! No danger thine:
Firm stand thy sons to watch the Rhine.

They stand, a hundred thousand strong,
Quick to avenge their country's wrong:
With filial love their bosoms swell:
They'll guard the sacred landmark well.
Dear Fatherland! No danger thine:
Firm stand thy sons to watch the Rhine.

And though in death our hopes decay,
The Rhine will own no foreign sway;
For rich with water as its flood
Is Germany with hero blood.
Dear Fatherland! No danger thine:
Firm stand thy sons to watch the Rhine

From yon blue sky are bending now,
The hero dead who hear our vow:
" As long as German hearts are free
The Rhine, the Rhine, shall German be."
Dear Fatherland! No danger thine:
Firm stand thy sons to watch the Rhine

" While flows one drop of German blood,
Or sword remains to guard thy flood,
While rifle rests in patriot's hand,
No foe shall tread thy sacred strand."
Dear Fatherland! No danger thine:
Firm stand thy sons to watch the Rhine.

Our oath resounds: the river flows;
In golden light our banner glows;
Our hearts will guard thy stream divine:
The Rhine! the Rhine! the German Rhine!
Dear Fatherland! No danger thine:
Firm stand thy sons to watch the Rhine.

MAX SCHNECKENBURGER.

THE WHITE-FOOTED DEER

IT was a hundred years ago,
  When, by the woodland ways,
The traveller saw the wild deer drink
  Or crop the birchen sprays.

Beneath a hill, whose rocky side
  O'erbrowed a grassy mead,
And fenced a cottage from the wind,
  A deer was wont to feed.

She only came when on the cliffs
  The evening moonlight lay,
And no man knew the secret haunts
  In which she walked by day.

White were her feet, her forehead showed
  A spot of silvery white,
That seemed to glimmer like a star
  In autumn's hazy night.

And here, when sang the whippoorwill,
  She cropped the sprouting leaves,
And here her rustling steps were heard
  On still October eves.

But when the broad midsummer moon
   Rose o'er that grassy lawn,
Beside the silver-footed deer
   There grazed a spotted fawn.

The cottage dame forbade her son
   To aim the rifle here;
" It were a sin," she said, " to harm
   Or fright that friendly deer.

" This spot has been my pleasant home
   Ten peaceful years and more;
And, ever, when the moonlight shines,
   She feeds before our door.

" The red-men say that here she walked
   A thousand moons ago;
They never raise the war-whoop here,
   And never twang the bow.

" I love to watch her as she feeds,
   And think that all is well
While such a gentle creature haunts
   The place in which we dwell."

The youth obeyed, and sought for game
   In forests far away,
Where, deep in silence and in moss,
   The ancient woodland lay.

But once, in autumn's golden time
    He ranged the wild in vain,
Nor roused the pheasant nor the deer,
    And wandered home again.

The crescent moon and crimson eve
    Shone with a mingling light;
The deer, upon the grassy mead,
    Was feeding full in sight.

He raised the rifle to his eye,
    And from the cliffs around
A sudden echo, shrill and sharp,
    Gave back its deadly sound.

Away, into the neighboring wood,
    The startled creature flew,
And crimson drops at morning lay
    Amid the glimmering dew.

Next evening shone the waxing moon
    As brightly as before;
The deer upon the grassy mead
    Was seen again no more.

But ere that crescent moon was old,
    By night the red-men came,
And burnt the cottage to the ground,
    And slew the youth and dame.

Now woods have overgrown the mead,
  And hid the cliffs from sight;
There shrieks the hovering hawk at noon,
  And prowls the fox at night.

WILLIAM CULLEN BRYANT.

MERCY

[From *Merchant of Venice*.]

T HE quality of mercy is not strained;
    It droppeth as the gentle rain from heaven
Upon the place beneath: it is twice blessed,—
It blesseth him that gives and him that takes:
'Tis mightiest in the mightiest; it becomes
The throned monarch better than his crown:
His sceptre shows the force of temporal power,
The attribute to awe and majesty,
Wherein doth sit the fear and dread of kings;
But mercy is above this sceptred sway,—
It is enthroned in the hearts of kings,
It is an attribute to God himself;
And earthly power doth then show likest God's,
When mercy seasons justice.

SHAKESPEARE.

PUCK AND THE FAIRY QUEEN

[From *Midsummer Night's Dream*.]

OVER hill, over dale,
    Thorough bush, thorough brier,
Over park, over pale,
    Thorough flood, thorough fire
I do wander everywhere.
Swifter than the moon's sphere;
And I serve the fairy queen,
To dew her orbs upon the green;
The cowslips tall her pensioners be:
In their gold coats spots you see;
These be rubies, fairy favors,
In those freckles live their savors:
I must go seek some dewdrops here,
And hang a pearl in every cowslip's ear.

                      SHAKESPEARE.

MAY

MAY shall make the world anew;
  Golden sun and silver dew,
Money minted in the sky,
Shall the earth's new garments buy.
May shall make the orchards bloom;
And the blossom's fine perfume
Shall set all the honey bees
Murmuring among the trees.
May shall make the bud appear
Like a jewel, crystal clear,
'Mid the leaves upon the limb
Where the robin lilts his hymn.
May shall make the wild flowers tell
Where the shining snow-flakes fell,
Just as tho' each snow-flake's heart,
By some secret magic art,
Were transmitted to a flower
In the sunlight and the shower.
Is there such another, pray,
Wonder-making month of May?

E. D. SHERMAN.

SEVENTH YEAR

THE NAME OF OLD GLORY

I

"OLD Glory! say, who
  By the ships and the crew,
And the long, blended ranks of the gray and the blue,—
Who gave you, Old Glory, the name that you bear
With such pride everywhere
As you cast yourself free to the rapturous air
And leap out full length, as we're wanting you to?
Who gave you that name with the ring of the same,
And the honor and fame so becoming to you?
Your stripes stroked in ripples of white and of red,
With your stars at their glittering beat overhead—
By day and by night
Their delightfullest light
Laughing down from their little square heaven of blue!
Who gave you the name of Old Glory? Say, who—
Who gave you the name of Old Glory?"
The old banner lifted, and faltering then,
In vague lisps and whispers falls silent again.

II

" Old Glory,—speak out!—we are asking about
How you happened to 'favor' a name, so to say,
That sounds as familiar and careless and gay
As we cheer it and shout in our wild, breezy way;

We, the crowd, every man of us calling you that,
We—Tom, Dick and Harry—each swinging his hat
And hurrahing ' Old Glory! ' like you were our kin,
When—Lord!—we all know we're as common as sin!
And yet it just seems like you humor us all,
And waft us our thanks, as we hail you and fall
Into line, with you over us waving us on
Where our glorified, sanctified betters have gone.
And this is the reason we're wanting to know
(And we're wanting it so!—
Where our own fathers went we are willing to go)
Who gave you the name of Old Glory—O-ho!—
Who gave you the name of Old Glory? "
The old flag unfurled with a billowy thrill
For an instant, then wistfully sighed and was still.

III

"Old Glory, the story we're wanting to hear
Is what the plain facts of your christening were,—
For your name—just to hear it,
Repeat it and cheer, it's a tang to the spirit
As salt as a tear;—
And seeing you fly, and the boys marching by,
There's a shout in the throat and a blur in the eye
And an aching to live for you always—or die,
If, dying, we still keep you waving on high.
And so, by our love
For you, floating above,
And the scars of all wars and the sorrows thereof,

Who gave you the name of Old Glory and why
Are we thrilled at the name of Old Glory? "
Then the old banner leaped like a sail in the blast,
And fluttered an audible answer at last.

IV

And it spake, with a shake of the voice, and it said:
" By the driven snow-white and the living blood-red
Of my bars, and the heaven of stars overhead—
By the symbol conjoined of them all, skyward cast,
As I float from the steeple or flap at the mast,
Or drop o'er the sod where the long grasses nod,—
My name is as old as the glory of God.
So I came by the name of Old Glory."

JAMES W. RILEY.

JOG ON, JOG ON*

[From *The Winter's Tale*.]

JOG on, jog on the foot-path way,
  And merrily hent† the stile-a,
A merry heart goes all the day,
  Your sad tires in a mile-a.

Your paltry money bags of gold—
  What need have we to stare for,
When little or nothing soon is told,
  And we have the less to care for.

Then cast away care, let sorrow cease,
  A fig for melancholy;
Let's laugh and sing, or, if you please,
  We'll frolic with sweet Dolly.

* First stanza by Shakespeare. Last two stanzas by un-
known author in " Antidote Against Melancholy," 1661.
  † Hent=take.

A SONG OF CLOVER

I WONDER what the Clover thinks,
  Intimate friend of Bob-o'-links,
Lover of Daisies slim and white,
Waltzer with Buttercups at night;
Keeper of Inn for travelling Bees,
Serving to them wine-dregs and lees,
Left by the Royal Humming Birds,
Who sip and pay with fine-spun words;
Fellow with all the lowliest,
Peer of the gayest and the best;
Comrade of winds, beloved of sun,
Kissed by the Dew-drops, one by one;
Prophet of Good-Luck mystery
By sign of four which few may see;
Symbol of Nature's magic zone,
One out of three, and three in one;
Emblem of comfort in the speech
Which poor men's babies early reach;
Sweet by the roadsides, sweet by rills,
Sweet in the meadows, sweet on hills,
Sweet in its white, sweet in its red,—
Oh, half its sweetness cannot be said;—
Sweet in its every living breath.
Sweetest, perhaps, at last, in death!
Oh! who knows what the Clover thinks?
No one! unless the Bob-o'-links!

                              " SAXE HOLM."

147

A SONG OF LOVE

SAY, what is the spell, when her fledglings are cheeping,
  That lures the bird home to her nest?
Or wakes the tired mother, whose infant is weeping,
  To cuddle and croon it to rest?
What the magic that charms the glad babe in her arms,
  Till it cooes with the voice of the dove?
'Tis a secret, and so let us whisper it low—
  And the name of the secret is Love!
            For I think it is Love,
            For I feel it is Love,
    For I'm sure it is nothing but Love!

Say, whence is the voice that when anger is burning,
  Bids the whirl of the tempest to cease?
That stirs the vexed soul with an aching—a yearning
  For the brotherly hand-grip of peace?
Whence the music that fills all our being—that thrills
  Around us, beneath, and above?
'Tis a secret: none knows how it comes, or it goes—
  But the name of the secret is Love!
            For I think it is Love,
            For I feel it is Love,
    For I'm sure it is nothing but Love!

Say, whose is the skill that paints valley and hill,
   Like a picture so fair to the sight?
That flecks the green meadow with sunshine and shadow,
   Till the little lambs leap with delight?
'Tis a secret untold to hearts cruel and cold,
   Though 'tis sung by the angels above,
In notes that ring clear for the ears that can hear—
   And the name of the secret is Love!
         For I think it is Love,
         For I feel it is Love,
   For I'm sure it is nothing but Love!

LEWIS CARROLL.

SCYTHE SONG

MOWERS, weary and brown, and blithe,
    What is the word methinks ye know,
Endless over-word that the Scythe
    Sings to the blades of the grass below?
Scythes that swing in the grass and clover,
    Something, still, they say as they pass;
What is the word that, over and over,
    Sings the Scythe to the flowers and grass?

Hush, ah, hush, the Scythes are saying,
    Hush, and heed not, and fall asleep;
Hush, they say to the grasses swaying,
    Hush, they sing to the clover deep!
Hush,—'tis the lullaby Time is singing—
    Hush, and heed, for all things pass.
Hush, ah, hush! and the Scythes are swinging
    Over the clover, over the grass!

ANDREW LANG.

AN INTERVIEW WITH MILES
STANDISH

I SAT one evening in my room,
  In that sweet hour of twilight
When blended thoughts, half light, half gloom,
  Throng through the spirit's skylight;
The flames by fits curled round the bars,
  Or up the chimney crinkled,
While embers dropped like falling stars,
  And in the ashes tinkled.

I sat and mused; the fire burned low,
  And, o'er my senses stealing,
Crept something of the ruddy glow
  That bloomed on wall and ceiling;
My pictures (they are very few,
  The heads of ancient wise men)
Smoothed down their knotted fronts and grew
  As rosy as excisemen.

My antique high-backed Spanish chair
  Felt thrills through wood and leather,
That had been strangers since whilere
  'Mid Andalusian heather,

The oak that built its sturdy frame
   His happy arms stretched over
The ox whose fortunate hide became
   The bottom's polished cover.

It came out in that famous bark,
   That brought our sires intrepid,
Capacious as another ark
   For furniture decrepit;
For, as that saved of bird and beast
   A pair for propagation,
So has the seed of these increased
   And furnished half the nation.

Kings sit, they say, in slippery seats;
   But those slant precipices
Of ice the northern voyager meets
   Less slippery are than this is;
To cling therein would pass the wit
   Of royal man or woman,
And whosoe'er can stay in it
   Is more or less than human.

I offer to all bores this perch,
   Dear well-intentioned people
With heads as void as week-day church,
   Tongues longer than the steeple;
To folks with missions, whose gaunt eyes
   See golden ages rising,—
Salt of the earth! in what queer Guys
   Thou'rt fond of crystallizing!

My wonder, then, was not unmixed
  With merciful suggestion,
When, as my roving eyes grew fixed
  Upon the chair in question,
I saw its trembling arms enclose
  A figure grim and rusty,
Whose doublet plain and plainer hose
  Were something worn and dusty.

Now even such men as Nature forms
  Merely to fill the street with,
Once turned to ghosts by hungry worms,
  Are serious things to meet with;
Your penitent spirits are no jokes,
  And though I'm not averse to
A quiet shade, even they are folks
  One cares not to speak first to.

Who knows, thought I, but he has come,
  By Charon kindly ferried,
To tell me of a mighty sum
  Behind my wainscot buried?
There is a buccaneerish air
  About that garb outlandish—
Just then the ghost drew up his chair
  And said, " My name is Standish.

" I come from Plymouth, deadly bored
  With toasts, and songs and speeches,
As long and flat as my old sword,
  As threadbare as my breeches:

They understand us Pilgrims! they,
  Smooth men with rosy faces,
Strength's knots and gnarls all pared away,
  And varnish in their places!

" We had some toughness in our grain,
  The eye to rightly see us is
Not just the one that lights the brain
  Of drawing-room Tyrtæuses:
They talk about their Pilgrim blood,
  Their birthright high and holy!
A mountain stream that ends in mud
  Methinks is melancholy.

" He had stiff knees, the Puritan,
  That were not good at bending;
The homespun dignity of man
  He thought was worth defending;
He did not with his pinchbeck ore,
  His country's shame forgotten,
Gild Freedom's coffin o'er and o'er,
  When all within was rotten.

" These loud ancestral boasts of yours,
  How can they else than vex us?
Where were your dinner orators
  When slavery grasped at Texas?
Dumb on his knees was every one
  That now is bold as Cæsar;
Mere pegs to hang an office on
  Such stalwart men as these are."

" Good sir," I said, " you seem much stirred;
    The sacred compromises "—

   .   .   .   .   .   .

Half rose the ghost, and half drew out
    The ghost of his old broadsword,
Then thrust it slowly back again,
    And said, with reverent gesture,
" No, Freedom, no! blood should not stain
    The hem of thy white vesture.

" I feel the soul in me draw near
    The mount of prophesying;
In this bleak wilderness I hear
    A John the Baptist crying;
Far in the east I see upleap
    The streaks of first forewarning,
And they who sowed the light shall reap
    The golden sheaves of morning.

" Child of our travail and our woe,
    Light in our day of sorrow,
Through my rapt spirit I foreknow
    The glory of thy morrow;
I hear great steps, that through the shade
    Draw nigher still and nigher,
And voices call like that which bade
    The prophet come up higher."

I looked, no form mine eyes could find,
    I heard the red cock crowing,
And through the window-chinks the wind
    A dismal tune was blowing;

Thought I, my neighbor Buckingham
Hath somewhat in him gritty,
Some Pilgrim-stuff that hates all sham,
And he will print my ditty.

JAMES RUSSELL LOWELL.

BANNOCKBURN

" SCOTS, wha hae wi' Wallace bled,
     Scots, wham Bruce has often led,
Welcome to your gory bed,
Or to glorious victory!

" Now's the day, and now's the hour;
See the front o' battle lour;
See approach proud Edward's power,—
Edward! chains and slavery!

" Wha will be a traitor knave?
Wha can fill a coward's grave?
Wha sae base as be a slave?
Traitor! coward! turn and flee!

" Wha for Scotland's king and law
Freedom's sword will strongly draw,
Freeman stand, or freeman fa',
Caledonia! on wi' me!

" By oppression's woes and pains!
By your sons in servile chains!
We will drain our dearest veins,
But they shall be—shall be free!

BANNOCKBURN

" Lay the proud usurpers low,
Tyrants fall in every foe!
Liberty's in every blow!
Forward! let us do or die! "

ROBERT BURNS.

FIDELITY

A BARKING sound the shepherd hears,
    A cry as of a dog or fox;
He halts and searches with his eyes
Among the scattered rocks:
And now at distance can discern
A stirring in a brake of fern;
And instantly a dog is seen,
Glancing through that covert green.

The dog is not of mountain breed;
Its motions, too, are wild and shy;
With something as the shepherd thinks,
Unusual in its cry:
Nor is there any one in sight
All round, in hollow or on height;
Nor shout, nor whistle strikes his ear;
What is the creature doing here?

It was a cove, a huge recess,
That keeps, till June, December's snow;
A lofty precipice in front,
A silent tarn below!
Far in the bosom of Helvellyn,
Remote from public road or dwelling,
Pathway, or cultivated land;
From trace of human foot or hand.

There sometimes doth a leaping fish
Send through the tarn a lonely cheer;
The crags repeat the raven's croak,
In symphony austere;
Thither the rainbow comes—the cloud—
And mists that spread the flying shroud;
And sunbeams; and the sounding blast,
That, if it could, would hurry past;
But that enormous barrier binds it fast.

Not free from boding thoughts, a while
The shepherd stood: then makes his way
O'er rocks and stones, following the dog
As quickly as he may;
Nor far had gone before he found
A human skeleton on the ground;
The appalled Discoverer with a sigh
Looks round, to learn the history.

From those abrupt and perilous rocks
The man had fallen, to that place of fear!
At length upon the shepherd's mind
It breaks, and all is clear:
He instantly recalled the name,
And who he was and whence he came;
Remembered, too, the very day
On which the traveller passed this way.

But hear a wonder, for whose sake
This lamentable tale I tell!
A lasting monument of words
This wonder merits well.

The dog which still was hovering nigh,
Repeating the same timid cry,
This dog, had been through three months' space
A dweller in that savage place.

Yes, proof was plain that, since the day
When this ill-fated traveller died,
The dog had watched about the spot,
Or by his master's side:
How nourished here through such long time
He knows, who gave that love sublime;
And gave that strength of feeling, great
Above all human estimate!

WORDSWORTH.

GOOD NAME IN MAN AND WOMAN

[From *Othello*.]

GOOD name in man and woman, dear my lord,
 Is the immediate jewel of their souls:
Who steals my purse, steals trash; 'tis something, nothing;
'Twas mine, 'tis his, and has been slave to thousands:
But he that filches from me my good name
Robs me of that which not enriches him
And makes me poor indeed.

SHAKESPEARE.

HOHENLINDEN

ON Linden when the sun was low,
    All bloodless lay the untrodden snow;
And dark as winter was the flow
Of Iser, rolling rapidly.

But Linden saw another sight
When the drum beat at dead of night,
Commanding fires of death to light
The darkness of her scenery.

By torch and trumpet fast arrayed,
Each horseman drew his battle blade,
And furious every charger neighed,
To join the dreadful revelry.

Then shook the hills with thunder riven,
Then rushed the steed to battle driven,
And louder than the bolts of heaven
Far flashed the red artillery.

But redder yet that light shall glow
On Linden's hills of stainèd snow,
And bloodier yet the current flow
Of Iser, rolling rapidly.

'Tis morn, but scarce yon level sun
Can pierce the war clouds, rolling dun,
Where furious Frank and fiery Hun
Shout in their sulphurous canopy.

The combat deepens. On, ye brave,
Who rush to glory, or the grave!
Wave Munich! all thy banners wave,
And charge with all thy chivalry!

Few, few, shall part where many meet!
The snow shall be their winding sheet,
And every turf beneath their feet
Shall be a soldier's sepulchre.

THOMAS CAMPBELL.

HYMN TO THE NORTH STAR

THE sad and solemn night
    Hath yet her multitude of cheerful fires;
The glorious host of light
    Walk the dark hemisphere till she retires;
All through her silent watches, gliding slow,
Her constellations come, and climb the heavens, and go.

Day, too, hath many a star
    To grace his gorgeous reign, as bright as they:
Through the blue fields afar,
    Unseen they follow in his flaming way:
Many a bright lingerer, as the eve grows dim,
Tells what a radiant troop arose and set with him.

And thou dost see them rise,
    Star of the Pole! and thou dost see them set.
Alone, in thy cold skies,
    Thou keep'st thy old unmoving station yet,
Nor join'st the dances of that glittering train,
Nor dipp'st thy virgin orb in the blue western main.

There at morn's rosy birth,
    Thou lookest meekly through the kindling air,
And eve, that round the earth
    Chases the day, beholds thee watching there;
There noontide finds thee, and the hour that calls
The shapes of polar flame to scale heaven's azure walls

Alike, beneath thine eye,
  The deeds of darkness and of light are done;
High toward the starlit sky
  Towns blaze, the smoke of battle blots the sun,
The night storm on a thousand hills is loud,
And the strong wind of day doth mingle sea and cloud.

On thy unaltering blaze
  The half-wrecked mariner, his compass lost,
Fixes his steady gaze,
  And steers, undoubting, to the friendly coast;
And they who stray in perilous wastes, by night,
Are glad when thou dost shine to guide their footsteps
    right.

And, therefore, bards of old,
  Sages and hermits of the solemn wood,
Did in thy beams behold
  A beauteous type of that unchanging good,
That bright eternal beacon, by whose ray
The voyager of time should shape his heedful way.

                                    WILLIAM CULLEN BRYANT.

THANATOPSIS

To him who, in the love of nature, holds
   Communion with her visible forms, she speaks
A various language: for his gayer hours
She has a voice of gladness, and a smile
And eloquence of beauty; and she glides
Into his darker musings, with a mild
And healing sympathy, that steals away
Their sharpness, ere he is aware. When thoughts
Of the last bitter hour come like a blight
Over thy spirit, and sad images
Of the stern agony, and shroud, and pall,
And breathless darkness, and the narrow house,
Make thee to shudder, and grow sick at heart,—
Go forth under the open sky, and list
To Nature's teachings, while from all around—
Earth and her waters, and the depths of air—
Comes a still voice:—Yet a few days and thee
The all-beholding sun shall see no more
In all his course; nor yet in the cold ground,
Where thy pale form was laid, with many tears,
Nor in the embrace of ocean, shall exist
Thy image. Earth, that nourished thee, shall claim
Thy growth, to be resolved to earth again;
And, lost each human trace, surrendering up
Thine individual being, shalt thou go

To mix forever with the elements,
To be a brother to the insensible rock
And to the sluggish clod, which the rude swain
Turns with his share and treads upon.   The oak
Shall send its roots abroad, and pierce thy mould.

Yet not to thine eternal resting-place
Shalt thou retire alone, nor couldst thou wish
Couch more magnificent.   Thou shalt lie down
With patriarchs of the infant world—with kings,
The powerful of the earth,—the wise, the good,
Fair forms, and hoary seers of ages past,
All in one mighty sepulchre.   The hills
Rock-ribbed, and ancient as the sun;—the vales
Stretching in pensive quietness between;
The venerable woods; rivers that move
In majesty, and the complaining brooks,
That make the meadows green; and, poured round all,
Old Ocean's gray and melancholy waste,—
Are but the solemn decorations all
Of the great tomb of man!   The golden sun,
The planets, all the infinite hosts of heaven,
Are shining on the sad abodes of death,
Through the still lapse of ages.   All that tread
The globe are but a handful to the tribes
That slumber in its bosom.   Take the wings
Of morning, pierce the Barcan wilderness,
Or lose thyself in the continuous woods
Where rolls the Oregon, and hears no sound
Save his own dashings—yet the dead are there:
And millions in those solitudes, since first

The flight of years began, have laid them down
In their last sleep—the dead reign there alone!
So shalt thou rest, and what if thou withdraw
In silence from the living; and no friend
Take note of thy departure? All that breathe
Will share thy destiny. The gay will laugh
When thou art gone, the solemn brood of care
Plod on, and each one as before shall chase
His favorite phantom; yet all these shall leave
Their mirth and their employments, and shall come
And make their bed with thee. As the long train
Of ages glides away, the sons of men,
The youth in life's green spring, and he who goes
In the full strength of years, matron and maid,
And the sweet babe, and the gray-headed man—
Shall one by one be gathered to thy side,
By those, who in their turn shall follow them.

So live that when thy summons comes to join
The innumerable caravan that moves
To that mysterious realm, where each shall take
His chamber in the silent halls of death,
Thou go not, like the quarry-slave at night,
Scourged to his dungeon, but, sustained and soothed
By an unfaltering trust, approach thy grave,
Like one who wraps the drapery of his couch
About him, and lies down to pleasant dreams.

WILLIAM CULLEN BRYANT.

THE ANTIQUITY OF FREEDOM

. . . . . .

O FREEDOM! thou art not, as poets dream,
    A fair young girl, with light and delicate limbs,
And wavy tresses gushing from the cap
With which the Roman master crowned his slave
When he took off the gyves. A bearded man,
Armed to the teeth, art thou; one mailèd hand
Grasps the broad shield, and one the sword; thy brow,
Glorious in beauty though it be, is scarred
With tokens of old wars; thy massive limbs
Are strong with struggling. Power at thee has launched
His bolts, and with his lightnings smitten thee;
They could not quench the life thou hast from heaven.
Merciless Power has dug thy dungeon deep,
And his swart armorers, by a thousand fires,
Have forged thy chain; yet while he deems thee bound,
The links are shivered, and the prison walls
Fall outward; terribly thou springest forth,
As springs the flame above a burning pile,
And shoutest to the nations, who return
Thy shoutings, while the pale oppressor flies.

. . . . . .

WILLIAM CULLEN BRYANT.

THE BATTLE OF THE BALTIC

OF Nelson and the North
   Sing the glorious day's renown,
When to battle fierce came forth
   All the might of Denmark's crown,
And her arms along the deep proudly shone:
   By each gun the lighted brand
   In a bold, determined hand,
      And the Prince of all the land
         Led them on.

Like leviathans afloat,
   Lay their bulwarks on the brine,
While the sign of battle flew
   On the lofty British line:
It was ten of April morn by the chime.
   As they drifted on their path,
   There was silence deep as death;
   And the boldest held his breath,
         For a time.

But the might of England flushed
   To anticipate the scene;
And her van the fleeter rushed
   O'er the deadly space between.

" Hearts of Oak ! " our captains cried ; when each gun
   From its adamantine lips
   Spread a death shade round the ships,
   Like the hurricane eclipse
       Of the sun.

Again ! again ! again !
   And the havoc did not slack,
Till a feeble cheer the Dane,
   To our cheering sent us back ;
Their shots along the deep slowly boom :—
   Then cease—and all is wail,
   As they strike the shattered sail,
   Or, in conflagration pale,
       Light the gloom.

     .   .   .   .   .   .

Now joy, old England, raise
   For the tidings of thy might,
By the festal cities blaze,
   Whilst the wine cup shines in light ;
And yet, amidst that joy and uproar,
   Let us think of them that sleep
   Full many a fathom deep
   By thy wild and stormy steep,
       Elsinore.

     .   .   .   .   .   .

THOMAS CAMPBELL.

THE CAVALRY CHARGE

OUR good steeds snuff the evening air,
   Our pulses with their purpose tingle;
The foeman's fires are twinkling there;
   He leaps to hear our sabres jingle.
       Halt!
Each carbine sent its whizzing ball:
Now cling! clang! forward all
      Into the fight!

Dash on beneath the smoking dome!
   Through level lightnings gallop nearer!
One look to Heaven! No thoughts of home;
   The guidons that we bear are dearer.
      Charge!
Cling! clang! forward all!
Heaven help those whose horses fall!
     Cut left and right!

They flee before our fierce attack!
   They fall! they spread in broken surges!
Now, comrades, bear our wounded back
   And leave the foeman to his dirges!
      Wheel!
The bugles sound the swift recall;
Cling! clang! backward all!
    Home, and good-night!

EDMUND CLARENCE STEDMAN.

THE CHARGE OF THE LIGHT BRIGADE

H ALF a league, half a league,
    Half a league onward,
All in the valley of Death
Rode the six hundred.
" Forward the Light Brigade!
Charge for the guns!" he said:
Into the valley of Death
Rode the six hundred.

" Forward the Light Brigade!"
Was there a man dismayed?
Not tho' the soldier knew
Some one had blunder'd:
Theirs not to make reply,
Theirs not to reason why,
Theirs but to do and die:
Into the valley of Death
Rode the six hundred.

Cannon to right of them,
Cannon to left of them,
Cannon in front of them
Volleyed and thunder'd;

Storm'd at with shot and shell,
Boldly they rode and well,
Into the jaws of Death,
Into the mouth of Hell,
Rode the six hundred.

Flashed all their sabres bare,
Flashed as they turned in air,
Sab'ring the gunners there,
Charging an army, while
All the world wondered:
Plunged in the battery smoke,
Right through the line they broke;
Cossack and Russian
Reeled from the sabre stroke
Shattered and sundered.
Then they rode back, but not,
Not the six hundred.

Cannon to right of them,
Cannon to left of them,
Cannon behind them
Volleyed and thundered;
Stormed at with shot and shell,
While horse and hero fell,
They that had fought so well,
Came thro' the jaws of Death,
Back from the mouth of Hell,
All that was left of them,
Left of six hundred.

When can their glory fade?
Oh, the wild charge they made!
All the world wondered.
Honor the charge they made!
Honor the Light Brigade,
Noble six hundred!

TENNYSON.

THE CROWDED STREET

L ET us move slowly through the street,
    Filled with an ever shifting train,
Amid the sound of steps that beat
    The murmuring walks like autumn rain.

How fast the flitting figures come!
    The mild, the fierce, the stony face,—
Some bright with thoughtless smiles, and some
    Where secret tears have left their trace.

They pass—to toil, to strive, to rest;
    To halls in which the feast is spread;
To chambers where the funeral guest
    In silence sits beside the dead.

And some to happy homes repair,
    Where children, pressing, cheek to cheek,
With mute caresses shall declare
    The tenderness they cannot speak.

And some who walk in calmness here,
    Shall shudder as they reach the door
Where one who made their dwelling dear,
    Its flower, its light, is seen no more.

Youth, with pale cheek and slender frame,
  And dreams of greatness in thine eye!
Go'st thou to build an early name,
  Or early in the task to die?

Keen son of trade, with eager brow!
  Who is now fluttering in thy snare?
Thy golden fortunes, tower they now,
  Or melt the glittering spires in air?

Who of this crowd to-night shall tread
  The dance till daylight gleam again?
Who sorrow o'er the untimely dead?
  Who writhe in throes of mortal pain?

Some, famine struck, shall think how long
  The cold, dark hours, how slow the light;
And some, who flaunt amid the throng,
  Shall hide in dens of shame to-night.

Each where his tasks or pleasures call,
  They pass and heed each other not.
There is who heeds, who holds them all
  In His large love and boundless thought.

These struggling tides of life, that seem
  In wayward, aimless course to tend,
Are eddies of the mighty stream
  That rolls to its appointed end.

          WILLIAM CULLEN BRYANT.

THE FINDING OF THE LYRE

THERE lay upon the ocean's shore
    What once a tortoise served to cover;
A year and more, with rush and roar,
    The surf had rolled it over,
Had played with it, and flung it by,
    As wind and weather might decide it,
Then tossed it high where sand-drifts dry
    Cheap burial might provide it.

It rested there to bleach or tan,
    The rains had soaked, the sun had burned it;
With many a ban the fisherman
    Had stumbled o'er and spurned it;
And there the fisher-girl would stay,
    Conjecturing with her brother
How in their play the poor estray
    Might serve some use or other.

So there it lay through wet and dry
    As empty as the last new sonnet,
Till by and by came Mercury,
    And, having mused upon it,
" Why here," cried he, " the thing of things
    In shape, material, and dimension!
Give it but strings, and, lo, it sings,
    A wonderful invention! "

So said, so done; the chords he strained,
   And, as his fingers o'er them hovered,
The shell disdained a soul had gained,
   The lyre had been discovered.
O empty world that round us lies,
   Dead shell, of soul and thought forsaken,
Brought we but eyes like Mercury's,
   In thee what songs should waken!

JAMES RUSSELL LOWELL.

THE NOBLE NATURE

IT is not growing like a tree
   In bulk, doth make man better be;
Or standing long an oak, three hundred year,
To fall a log at last, dry, bald, and sear.
A lily of a day
Is fairer far in May,
Although it fall and die that night,—
It was the plant and flower of Light.
In small proportions we just beauties see;
And in short measures life may perfect be.

BEN JONSON.

THE PATRIOT

IT was roses, roses all the way,
  With myrtle mixed in my path like mad:
The house roofs seemed to heave and sway,
  The church spires flamed, such flags they had
A year ago on this very day.

The air broke into a mist with bells,
  The old wall rocked with the crowd and cries.
Had I said, " Good folk, mere noise repels—
  But give me your sun from yonder skies! "
They had answered, " And afterward, what else? "

Alack, it was I who leaped at the sun
  To give it to my loving friends to keep;
Naught man could do, have I left undone:
  And you see my harvest, what I reap
This very day, now a year is run.

There's nobody on the housetops now—
  Just a palsied few at the windows set;
For the best of the sight is, all allow,
  At the Shambles Gate—or, better yet,
By the very scaffold's foot, I trow.

I go in the rain, and, more than needs,
   A rope cuts both my wrists behind;
And I think, by the feel, my forehead bleeds,
   For they fling, whoever has a mind,
Stones at me for my year's misdeeds.

Thus I entered, and thus I go!
   In triumphs, people have dropped down dead.
" Paid by the world, what dost thou owe
   Me? "—God might question; now instead,
'Tis God shall repay: I am safer so.

               ROBERT BROWNING.

THE RAINY DAY

THE day is cold, and dark, and dreary:
   It rains, and the wind is never weary;
  The vine still clings to the mouldering wall,
  But at every gust the dead leaves fall,
And the day is dark and dreary.

My life is cold, and dark, and dreary;
It rains, and the wind is never weary;
  My thoughts still cling to the mouldering Past,
  But the hopes of youth fall thick in the blast,
And the days are dark and dreary.

Be still, sad heart! and cease repining;
Behind the clouds is the sun still shining;
  Thy fate is the common fate of all,
  Into each life some rain must fall,
Some days must be dark and dreary.

LONGFELLOW.

TO A WATERFOWL

WHITHER, 'midst falling dew,
  While glow the heavens with the last steps of day,
Far, through their rosy depths, dost thou pursue
  Thy solitary way?

Vainly the fowler's eye
  Might mark thy distant flight to do thee wrong,
As, darkly painted on the crimson sky,
  Thy figure floats along.

Seek'st thou the plashy brink
  Of weedy lake, or marge of river wide,
Or where the rocking billows rise and sink
  On the chafed ocean's side?

There is a power whose care
  Teaches thy way along that pathless coast—
The desert and illimitable air—
  Lone wandering, but not lost.

All day thy wings have fanned,
  At that far height, the cold, thin atmosphere,
Yet stoop not weary, to the welcome land,
  Though the dark night is near.

And soon that toil shall end;
 Soon shalt thou find a summer home, and rest,
And scream among thy fellows; reeds shall bend
 Soon, o'er thy sheltered nest.

Thou'rt gone, the abyss of heaven
 Hath swallowed up thy form; yet, on my heart
Deeply has sunk the lesson thou hast given,
 And shall not soon depart.

He who from zone to zone,
 Guides through the boundless sky thy certain flight,
In the long way that I must tread alone,
 Will lead my steps aright.

WILLIAM CULLEN BRYANT.

THE YANKEE GIRL

SHE sings at her wheel at that low cottage door,
  Which the long evening shadow is stretching before,
With a music as sweet as the music which seems
Breathed softly and faint in the ear of our dreams!

How brilliant and mirthful the light of her eye,
Like a star glancing out from the blue of the sky!
And lightly and freely her dark tresses play
O'er a brow and a bosom as lovely as they!

Who comes in his pride to that low cottage door,—
The haughty and rich to the humble and poor?
'Tis the great Southern planter,—the master who waves
His whip of dominion o'er hundreds of slaves.

" Nay, Ellen,—for shame! Let those Yankee fools spin,
Who would pass for our slaves with a change of their
    skin;
Let them toil as they will at the loom or the wheel,
Too stupid for shame, and too vulgar to feel!

" But thou art too lovely and precious a gem
To be bound by their burdens and sullied by them,—
For shame, Ellen, shame,—cast thy bondage aside,
And away to the South, as my blessing and pride.

" Oh, come where no winter thy footsteps can wrong,
But where flowers are blossoming all the year long,
Where the shade of the palm tree is over my home,
And the lemon and orange are white in their bloom!

" Oh, come to my home, where my servants shall all
Depart at thy bidding and come at thy call;
They shall heed thee as mistress with trembling and awe,
And each wish of thy heart shall be felt as a law."

Oh, could ye have seen her, that pride of our girls—
Arise and cast back the dark wealth of her curls,
With a scorn in her eye which the gazer could feel,
And a glance like the sunshine that flashes on steel!

" Go back, haughty Southron! thy treasures of gold
Are dim with the blood of the hearts thou hast sold;
Thy home may be lovely, but around it I hear
The crack of the whip and the footsteps of fear!

" And the sky of thy South may be brighter than ours,
And greener thy landscapes, and fairer thy flowers;
But dearer the blast round our mountains which raves,
Than the sweet summer zephyr which breathes over
    slaves!

" Full low at thy bidding thy negroes may kneel,
With the iron of bondage on spirit and heel;
Yet know that the Yankee girl sooner would be
In fetters with them, than in freedom with thee!"

JOHN G. WHITTIER.

THE PAGEANT

OUR revels now are ended: These our actors,
   As I foretold you, were all spirits, and
  Are melted, into air, into thin air:
And, like the baseless fabric of this vision,
The cloud-capp'd towers, the gorgeous palaces,
The solemn temples, the great globe itself,
Yea, all which it inherit, shall dissolve;
And, like this insubstantial pageant faded,
Leave not a rack behind. We are such stuff
As dreams are made of, and our little life
Is rounded with a sleep.

SHAKESPEARE.

WHILE SHEPHERDS WATCHED THEIR
FLOCKS BY NIGHT

WHILE shepherds watched their flocks by night,
    All seated on the ground,
The angel of the Lord came down,
And glory shone around.

" Fear not," said he, for mighty dread
Had seized their troubled mind;
" Glad tidings of great joy I bring
To you and all mankind.

" To you in David's town this day,
Is born of David's line
A Saviour, who is Christ the Lord,
And this shall be the sign.

" The heavenly babe you there shall find
To human view displayed,
All meanly wrapped in swaddling bands,
And in a manger laid."

Thus spake the seraph, and forthwith
Appeared a shining throng
Of angels praising God, and thus
Addressed their joyful song:

" All glory be to God on high,
And to the earth be peace!
Good-will henceforth from heaven to men
Begin, and never cease."

NAHUM TATE.

WOLSEY'S FALL

[From *Henry VIII*.]

FAREWELL! a long farewell to all my greatness!
    This is the state of man: today he puts forth
The tender leaves of hope, to-morrow blossoms,
And bears his blushing honors thick upon him;
The third day comes a frost, a killing frost;
And—when he thinks, good easy man, full surely
His greatness is a-ripening—nips his root,
And then he falls, as I do. I have ventur'd,
Like little wanton boys that swim on bladders,
This many summers in a sea of glory,
But far beyond my depth; my high blown pride
At length broke under me; and now has left me,
Weary and old with service, to the mercy
Of a rude stream, that must forever hide me.
Vain pomp and glory of this world, I hate ye!
I feel my heart new-opened. O! how wretched
Is that poor man that hangs on princes' favors!
There is, betwixt that smile we would aspire to,
That sweet aspect of princes, and their ruin,
More pangs and fears than wars or women have;
And when he falls, he falls like Lucifer,
Never to hope again.

SHAKESPEARE.

EIGHTH YEAR

THE ANGLER'S REVEILLE

[From *The Toiling of Felix*.]

WHAT time the rose of dawn is laid across the lips
    of night,
And all the drowsy little stars have fallen asleep in light;
'Tis then a wandering wind awakes, and runs from tree
    to tree,
And borrows words from all the birds to sound the
    reveille.

      This is the carol the Robin throws
        Over the edge of the valley;
      Listen how boldly it flows,
        Sally on sally:
            Tirra-lirra,
            Down the river,
            Laughing water
            All a-quiver.
            Day is near,
            Clear, clear.
            Fish are breaking,
            Time for waking.
            Tup, tup, tup!
            Do you hear?
            All clear—
            Wake up!

The phantom flood of dreams has ebbed and vanished
    with the dark,
And like a dove the heart forsakes the prison of the ark;
Now forth she fares through friendly woods and diamond-
    fields of dew,
While every voice cries out "Rejoice!" as if the world
    were new.

        This is the ballad the Bluebird sings,
            Unto his mate replying,
        Shaking the tune from his wings
            While he is flying:

            Surely, surely, surely,
                Life is dear
                Even here.
                Blue above,
                You to love,
            Purely, purely, purely.

There's wild azalea on the hill, and roses down the dell,
And just one spray of lilac still a-bloom beside the well;
The columbine adorns the rocks, the laurel buds grow
    pink,
Along the stream white arums gleam, and violets bend
    to drink.

This is the song of the Yellowthroat,
  Fluttering gaily beside you;
Hear how each voluble note
  Offers to guide you:

> *Which way, sir?*
> *I say, sir,*
> *Let me teach you,*
> *I beseech you!*
> *Are you wishing*
> *Jolly fishing?*
> *This way, sir!*
> *I'll teach you.*

Then come, my friend, forget your foes, and leave your
  fears behind,
And wander forth to try your luck, with cheerful, quiet
  mind;
For be your fortune great or small, you'll take what
  God may give,
And all the day your heart shall say, " 'Tis luck enough
  to live."

This is the song the Brown Thrush flings
  Out of his thicket of roses;
Hark how it warbles and rings,
  Mark how it closes:

Luck, luck,
What luck?
Good enough for me!
I'm alive, you see.
Sun shining,
No repining;
Never borrow
Idle sorrow;
Drop it!
Cover it up!
Hold your cup!
Joy will fill it,
Don't spill it,
Steady, be ready,
Good luck!

HENRY VAN DYKE.

BUGLE SONG

THE splendor falls on castle walls,
   And snowy summits old in story:
The long light shakes across the lakes,
And the wild cataract leaps in glory.
Blow, bugle, blow, set the wild echoes flying,
Blow, bugle; answer, echoes, dying, dying, dying.

Oh, hark, oh, hear! how thin and clear,
And thinner, clearer, farther going!
Oh, sweet and far, from cliff and scar,
The horns of Elfland faintly blowing!
Blow, let us hear the purple glens replying:
Blow, bugle; answer, echoes, dying, dying, dying.

Oh, love, they die in yon rich sky,
They faint on hill or field or river:
Our echoes roll from soul to soul,
And grow forever and forever.
Blow, bugle, blow, set the wild echoes flying,
And answer, echoes, answer, dying, dying, dying.

TENNYSON.

A FAREWELL

FLOW down, cold rivulet, to the sea,
    Thy tribute wave deliver:
No more by thee my steps shall be,
    Forever and forever.

Flow, softly flow, by lawn and lea,
    A rivulet, then a river:
Nowhere by thee my steps shall be,
    Forever and forever.

But here will sigh thy alder tree,
    And here thy aspen shiver;
And here by thee will hum the bee,
    Forever and forever.

A thousand suns will stream on thee,
    A thousand moons will quiver;
But not by thee my steps shall be,
    Forever and forever.

                              TENNYSON.

A FOREST HYMN

THE groves were God's first temples. Ere man learned
    To hew the shaft, and lay the architrave,
And spread the roof above them,—ere he framed
The lofty vault, to gather and roll back
The sound of anthems; in the darkling wood,
Amidst the cool and silence, he knelt down,
And offered to the Mightiest solemn thanks
And supplication. For his simple heart
Might not resist the sacred influences
Which, from the stilly twilight of the place,
And from the gray old trunks that high in heaven
Mingled their mossy boughs, and from the sound
Of the invisible breath that swayed at once
All their green tops, stole over him, and bowed
His spirit with the thought of boundless power
And inaccessible majesty. Ah, why
Should we, in the world's riper years, neglect
God's ancient sanctuaries, and adore
Only among the crowd, and under roofs
That our frail hands have raised? Let me, at least,
Here in the shadow of this aged wood,
Offer one hymn,—thrice happy if it find
Acceptance in his ear.

Father, thy hand
Hath reared these venerable columns, thou
Didst weave this verdant roof. Thou didst look down
Upon the naked earth, and forthwith rose
All these fair ranks of trees. They in thy sun
Budded, and shook their green leaves in thy breeze,
And shot towards heaven. The century-living crow,
Whose birth was in their tops, grew old and died
Among their branches, till at last they stood,
As now they stand, massy and tall and dark,
Fit shrine for humble worshipper to hold
Communion with his Maker. These dim vaults,
These winding aisles, of human pomp and pride
Report not. No fantastic carvings show
The boast of our vain race to change the form
Of thy fair works. But thou art here,—thou fill'st
The solitude. Thou art in the soft winds
That run along the summit of these trees
In music; thou art in the cooler breath
That from the inmost darkness of the place
Comes, scarcely felt; the barky trunks, the ground,
The fresh, moist ground, are all instinct with thee.
Here is continual worship;—nature, here,
In the tranquillity that thou dost love,
Enjoys thy presence. Noiselessly around,
From perch to perch, the solitary bird
Passes; and yon clear spring, that, midst its herbs,
Wells softly forth, and wandering steeps the roots
Of half the mighty forest, tells no tale
Of all the good it does. Thou hast not left
Thyself without a witness, in these shades,

Of thy perfections.   Grandeur, strength, and grace
Are here to speak of thee.   This mighty oak,—
By whose immovable stem I stand and seem
Almost annihilated,—not a prince,
In all that proud old world beyond the deep,
E'er wore his crown as loftily as he
Wears the green coronal of leaves with which
Thy hand has graced him.   Nestled at his root
Is beauty, such as blooms not in the glare
Of the broad sun.   That delicate forest flower
With scented breath, and look so like a smile,
Seems, as it issues from the shapeless mould,
An emanation of the indwelling Life,
A visible token of the upholding Love,
That are the soul of this wide universe.

My heart is awed within me when I think
Of the great miracle that still goes on,
In silence round me,—the perpetual work
Of thy creation, finished, yet renewed
Forever.   Written on thy works I read
The lesson of thy own eternity.
Lo! all grow old and die; but see again,
How on the faltering footsteps of decay
Youth presses,—ever gay and beautiful youth
In all its beautiful forms.   These lofty trees
Wave not less proudly that their ancestors
Moulder beneath them.   O, there is not lost
One of Earth's charms! upon her bosom yet,
After the flight of untold centuries,
The freshness of her far beginning lies,

And yet shall lie. Life mocks the idle hate
Of his arch enemy, Death,— yea, seats himself
Upon the tyrant's throne, the sepulchre,
And of the triumphs of his ghastly foe
Makes his own nourishment. For he came forth
From thy own bosom, and shall have no end.

   There have been holy men who hid themselves
Deep in the woody wilderness, and gave
Their lives to thought and prayer, till they outlived
The generation born with them, nor seemed
Less aged than the hoary trees and rocks
Around them;—and there have been holy men
Who deemed it were not well to pass life thus.
But let me often to these solitudes
Retire, and in thy presence reassure
My feeble virtue. Here its enemies,
The passions, at thy plainer footsteps shrink
And tremble and are still. O God! when thou
Dost scare the world with tempests, set on fire
The heavens with falling thunderbolts, or fill,
With all the waters of the firmament,
The swift dark whirlwind that uproots the woods
And drowns the villages; when at thy call,
Uprises the great deep and throws himself
Upon the continent, and overwhelms
Its cities,—who forgets not, at the sight
Of these tremendous tokens of thy power,
His pride, and lays his strifes and follies by?
Oh, from these sterner aspects of thy face
Spare me and mine, nor let us need the wrath

Of the mad unchainèd elements to teach
Who rules them.   Be it ours to meditate,
In these calm shades, thy milder majesty,
And to the beautiful order of thy works
Learn to conform the order to our lives.

WILLIAM CULLEN BRYANT.

ALICE BRAND

I

MERRY it is in the good greenwood
  When the mavis and merle are singing,
When the deer sweeps by, and the hounds are in cry,
  And the hunter's horn is ringing.

" O Alice Brand, my native land
  Is lost for love of you;
And we must hold by wood and wold,
  As outlaws wont to do.

" O Alice, 'twas all for thy locks so bright,
  And 'twas all for thine eye so blue,
That on the night of our luckless flight,
  Thy brother bold I slew.

" Now I must teach to hew the beech
  The hand that held the glaive,
For leaves to spread our lowly bed,
  And stakes to fence our cave.

" And for vest of pall, thy fingers small,
  That wont on harp to stray,
A cloak must shear from the slaughter'd deer,
  To keep the cold away."—

" O Richard! if my brother died,
　'Twas but a fatal chance;
For darkling was the battle tried,
　And fortune sped the lance.

" If pall and vair no more I wear,
　Nor thou the crimson sheen,
As warm, we'll say, is the russet gray,
　As gay the forest green.

And, Richard, if our lot be hard,
　And lost my native land,
Still Alice has her own Richard,
　And he his Alice Brand."

II

'Tis merry, 'tis merry, in good greenwood,
　So blithe Lady Alice is singing;
On the beech's pride and oak's brown side,
　Lord Richard's axe is ringing.

Up spoke the moody Elfin King,
　Who won'd within the hill,—
Like wind in the porch of a ruined church,
　His voice was ghostly shrill.

" Why sounds yon stroke on beech and oak,
　Our moonlight circle's screen?
Or who comes here to chase the deer,
　Beloved of our Elfin Queen?

Or who may dare on wold to wear
    The fairies' fatal green?

" Up, Urgan, up! to yon mortal hie,
    For thou were christened man:
For cross or sign thou wilt not fly,
    For mutter'd word or ban.

" Lay on him the curse of the withered heart,
    The curse of the sleepless eye;
Till he wish and pray that his life would part,
    Nor yet find leave to die."

III

'Tis merry, 'tis merry, in good greenwood,
    Though the birds have stilled their singing;
The evening blaze doth Alice raise,
    And Richard is fagots bringing.

Up Urgan starts, that hideous dwarf,
    Before Lord Richard stands,
And as he cross'd and bless'd himself,
" I fear not sign," quoth the grisly elf,
    " That is made with bloody hands."

But out then spoke she, Alice Brand,
    That woman, void of fear,—
" And if there's blood upon his hand,
    'Tis but the blood of deer."—

" Now loud thou liest, thou bold of mood!
   It cleaves unto his hand,
The stain of thy own kindly blood,
   The blood of Ethert Brand."

Then forward stepped she, Alice Brand,
   And made the holy sign,—
" And if there's blood on Richard's hand,
   A spotless hand is mine.

" And I conjure thee, Demon elf,
   By Him whom demons fear,
To show us whence thou art thyself,
   And what thine errand here? "—

IV

" 'Tis merry, 'tis merry, in Fairyland,
   When fairy birds are singing,
When the court doth ride by their monarch's side,
   With bit and bridle ringing:

" And gaily shines the Fairyland,—
   But all is glistening show,
Like the idle gleam that December's beam
   Can dart on ice and snow.

" And fading, like that varied gleam,
   Is our inconstant shape,
Who now like knight and lady seem,
   And now like dwarf and ape.

" It was between the night and day,
    When the Fairy King has power,
That I sunk down in a sinful fray,
And, 'twixt life and death, was snatched away,
    To the joyless Elfin bower.

" But wist I of a woman bold,
    Who thrice my brow durst sign,
I might regain my mortal mould,
    As fair a form as thine."

She crossed him once—she crossed him twice—
    The lady was so brave;
The fouler grew his goblin hue,
    The darker grew the cave.

She crossed him thrice, that lady bold!
    He rose beneath her hand
The fairest knight on Scottish mould,
    Her brother, Ethert Brand!

Merry it is in good greenwood,
    When the mavis and merle are singing;
    But merrier were they in Dunfermline gray
    When all the bells were ringing.

                                    SIR WALTER SCOTT.

ANTONY'S EULOGY ON CÆSAR

FRIENDS, Romans, and countrymen, lend me your
        ears;
I come to bury Cæsar, not to praise him.
The evil that men do lives after them,
The good is oft interred with their bones;
So let it be with Cæsar.   The noble Brutus
Hath told you Cæsar was ambitious:
If it were so, it was a grievous fault,
And grievously hath Cæsar answer'd it.
Here, under leave of Brutus and the rest—
For Brutus is an honorable man;
So are they all, all honorable men—
Come I to speak in Cæsar's funeral.
He was my friend, faithful and just to me:
But Brutus says he was ambitious;
And Brutus is an honorable man.
He hath brought many captives home to Rome,
Whose ransom did the general coffers fill:
Did this in Cæsar seem ambitious?
When that the poor have cried, Cæsar hath wept:
Ambition should be made of sterner stuff:
Yet Brutus says he was ambitious;
And Brutus is an honorable man.
You all did see that on the Lupercal

I thrice presented him a kingly crown,
Which he did thrice refuse. Was this ambition?
Yet Brutus says he was ambitious;
And, sure, he is an honorable man.
I speak not to disprove what Brutus spoke,
But here I am to speak what I do know.
You all did love him once, not without cause:
What cause withholds you, then, to mourn for him?
O judgment! thou art fled to brutish beasts,
And men have lost their reason.—Bear with me;
My heart is in the coffin there with Cæsar,
And I must pause till it come back to me.

.   .   .   .   .   .

But yesterday the word of Cæsar might
Have stood against the world: now lies he there,
And none so poor to do him reverence.
O master! if I were dispos'd to stir
Your hearts and minds to mutiny and rage,
I should do Brutus wrong, and Cassius wrong,
Who, you all know, are honorable men.
I will not do them wrong: I rather choose
To wrong the dead, to wrong myself, and you,
Than I will wrong such honorable men.
But here's a parchment with the seal of Cæsar;
I found it in his closet, 'tis his will:
Let but the commons hear his testament—
Which, pardon me, I do not mean to read—
And they would go and kiss dead Cæsar's wounds,
And dip their napkins in his sacred blood,
Yea, beg a hair of him for memory,
And, dying, mention it within their wills,

Bequeathing it as a rich legacy
Unto their issue.

.   .   .   .   .   .

Have patience, gentle friends; I must not read it;
It is not meet you know how Cæsar lov'd you.
You are not wood, you are not stones, but men;
And, being men, hearing the will of Cæsar,
It will inflame you, it will make you mad:
'Tis good you know not that you are his heirs;
For, if you should, O, what would come of it!

.   .   .   .   .   .

Will you be patient? will you stay awhile?
I have o'ershot myself to tell you of it.
I fear I wrong the honorable men
Whose daggers have stabbed Cæsar: I do fear it.

.   .   .   .   .   .

You will compel me then to read the will?
Then make a ring about the corpse of Cæsar,
And let me show you him that made the will.
Shall I descend? and will you give me leave?

.   .   .   .   .   .

Nay, press not so upon me; stand far off.

.   .   .   .   .   .

If you have tears, prepare to shed them now.
You all do know this mantle: I remember
The first time ever Cæsar put it on;
'Twas on a summer's evening, in his tent,
That day he overcame the Nervii:
Look! in this place ran Cassius' dagger through:
See! what a rent the envious Casca made:
Through this the well-beloved Brutus stabbed;

And as he plucked his cursed steel away,
Mark how the blood of Cæsar followed it,
As rushing out of doors, to be resolved
If Brutus so unkindly knock'd, or no;
For Brutus, as you know, was Cæsar's angel:
Judge, O you gods, how dearly Cæsar lov'd him!
This was the most unkindest cut of all:
For when the noble Cæsar saw him stab,
Ingratitude, more strong than traitors' arms,
Quite vanquished him: then burst his mighty heart;
And, in his mantle muffling up his face,
Even at the base of Pompey's statua,
Which all the while ran blood, great Cæsar fell.
O, what a fall was there, my countrymen!
Then I, and you, and all of us fell down,
Whilst bloody treason flourished over us.
O! now you weep; and, I perceive, you feel
The dint of pity: these are gracious drops.
Kind souls! what! weep you when you but behold
Our Cæsar's vesture wounded?   Look you here,
Here is himself, marred, as you see, with traitors.

.   .   .   .   .   .

Stay, countrymen.

.   .   .   .   .   .

Good friends, sweet friends, let me not stir you up
To such a sudden flood of mutiny.
They that have done this deed are honorable:
What private griefs they have, alas! I know not,
That made them do it: they are wise and honorable,
And will, no doubt, with reasons answer you.
I come not, friends, to steal away your hearts:

I am no orator, as Brutus is;
But, as you know me all, a plain, blunt man,
That love my friend; and that they know full well
That gave me public leave to speak of him.
For I have neither wit, nor words, nor worth,
Action, nor utterance, nor the power of speech,
To stir men's blood: I only speak right on;
I tell you that which you yourselves do know;
Show you sweet Cæsar's wounds, poor, poor dumb mouths,
And bid them speak for me: but were I Brutus,
And Brutus Antony, there were an Antony
Would ruffle up your spirits and put a tongue
In every wound of Cæsar, that should move
The stones of Rome to rise and mutiny.

· · · · ·

Yet hear me, countrymen; yet hear me speak.

· · · · · ·

Why, friends, you go to do you know not what.
Wherein hath Cæsar thus deserved your loves?
Alas, you know not:—I must tell you, then.
You have forgot the will I told you of.

· · · · · ·

Here is the will, and under Cæsar's seal.
To every Roman citizen he gives,
To every several man, seventy-five drachmas.

· · · · · ·

Hear me with patience.

· · · · · ·

Moreover, he hath left you all his walks,
His private arbors, and new-planted orchards,

On this side Tiber; he hath left them you,
And to your heirs forever; common pleasures,
To walk abroad, and recreate yourselves.
Here was a Cæsar! when comes such another?

SHAKESPEARE.

AN ORDER FOR A PICTURE

OH, good painter, tell me true,
    Has your hand the cunning to draw
Shapes of things that you never saw?
Aye? Well, here is an order for you.

Woods and cornfields, a little brown,—
The picture must not be over bright,—
Yet all in the golden and gracious light
Of a cloud, when the summer sun is down.
Alway and alway, night and morn,
Woods upon woods, with fields of corn
Lying between them, not quite sere,
And not in the full, thick, leafy bloom,
When the wind can hardly find breathing room
Under their tassels,—cattle near,
Biting shorter the short green grass,
And a hedge of sumac and sassafras,
With bluebirds twittering all around,—
(Ah, good painter, can you paint sound!)—
These and the house where I was born,
Low and little, and black and old,
With children, many as it can hold,
All at the windows, open wide,—
Heads and shoulders all outside,
And fair young faces all ablush:

Perhaps you may have seen, some day,
Roses crowding the selfsame way,
Out of a wilding, wayside bush.

Listen closer. When you have done
With woods and cornfields and grazing herds,
A lady, the loveliest ever the sun
Looked down upon you must paint for me:
Oh, if I could make you see
The clear blue eyes, the tender smile,
The sovereign sweetness, the gentle grace,
The woman's soul, and the angel's face
That are beaming on me all the while,
I need not speak these foolish words:
Yet one word tells you all I would say,—
She is my mother: you will agree
That all the rest may be thrown away.

Two little urchins at her knee
You must paint, sir, one like me,—
The other with a clearer brow,
And the light of his adventurous eyes
Flashing with boldest enterprise:
At ten years old he went to sea,—
God knoweth if he be living now,—
He sailed in the good ship *Commodore,*
Nobody ever crossed her track
To bring us news, and she never came back.
Ah, it is twenty long years and more
Since that old ship went out of the bay
With my great hearted brother on her deck:
I watched him till he shrank to a speck,

And his face was toward me all the way.
Bright his hair was, a golden brown,
The time we stood at our mother's knee:
That beauteous head if it did go down,
Carried sunshine into the sea!
Out in the fields one summer night
We were together, half afraid
Of the corn leaves rustling, and of the shade
Of the high hills, stretching so still and far,—
Loitering till after the low little light
Of the candle shone through the open door,
And over the hay-stack's pointed top,
All of a tremble and ready to drop,
The first half hour, the great yellow star,
That we, with staring, ignorant eyes,
Had often and often watched to see
Propped and held in its place in the skies
By the fork of a tall red mulberry tree,
Which close in the edge of our flaxfield grew,—
Dead at the top,—just one branch full
Of leaves, notched round, and lined with wool,
From which it tenderly shook the dew
Over our heads, when we came to play
In its handbreath of shadow, day after day.
Afraid to go home, sir; for one of us bore
A nestful of speckled and thin-shelled eggs,—
The other, a bird, held fast by the legs,
Not so big as a straw of wheat:
The berries we gave her she wouldn't eat,
But cried and cried, till we held her bill,
So slim and shining to keep her still.

At last we stood at our mother's knee
Do you think, sir, if you try,
You can paint the look of a lie?
If you can, pray have the grace
To put it solely in the face
Of the urchin that is likest me:
I think 'twas solely mine, indeed:
But that's no matter, paint it so;
The eyes of our mother (take good heed)—
Look not on the nestful of eggs,
Nor the fluttering bird, held so fast by the legs,
But straight through our faces down to our lies,
And, oh, with such injured, reproachful surprise!
I felt my heart bleed where that glance went, as
    though
A sharp blade struck through it.
    You, sir, know
That you on the canvas are to repeat
Things that are fairest, things most sweet,—
Woods and cornfields and mulberry-tree,—
The mother,—the lads, with their bird, at her
    knee:
But, oh, that look of reproachful woe!
High as the heavens your name I'll shout,
If you paint me the picture, and leave that out.

ALICE CARY.

THE BELLS

I

HEAR the sledges with the bells,—
    Silver bells!
What a world of merriment their melody foretells!
  How they tinkle, tinkle, tinkle,
    In the icy air of night!
  While the stars that oversprinkle
  All the heavens seem to twinkle
    With a crystalline delight,—
  Keeping time, time, time,
  In a sort of Runic rhyme,
To the tintinnabulation that so musically wells
    From the bells, bells, bells, bells,
From the jingling and the tinkling of the bells.
    Bells, bells, bells,—

II

Hear the mellow wedding bells,—
    Golden bells!
What a world of happiness their harmony foretells!
  Through the balmy air of night
  How they ring out their delight!
From the molten-golden notes,
    And all in tune,

What a liquid ditty floats
To the turtle-dove that listens, while she gloats
  On the moon!
 Oh, from out the sounding cells,
 What a gush of euphony wells!
   How it swells!
   How it dwells
  On the Future! how it tells
  Of the rapture that impels
To the swinging and the ringing
 Of the bells, bells, bells,
  Of the bells, bells, bells, bells,
   Bells, bells, bells,—
To the rhyming and the chiming of the bells.

III

Hear the loud alarum bells,—
   Brazen bells!
What a tale of terror now their turbulency tells!
 In the startled ear of night
 How they scream out their affright!
  Too much horrified to speak,
  They can only shriek, shriek,
   Out of tune,
In a clamorous appealing to the mercy of the fire,
In a mad expostulation with the deaf and frantic fire,
 Leaping higher, higher, higher,
 With a desperate desire,
  And a resolute endeavor,

Now—now to sit or never,
By the side of the pale-faced moon.
  O, the bells, bells, bells,
    What a tale their terror tells
          Of despair!
    How they clang and clash and roar!
    What a horror they outpour
On the bosom of the palpitating air!
        Yet the ear it fully knows,
          By the twanging,
          And the clanging,
        How the danger ebbs and flows;
        Yet the ear distinctly tells,
          In the jangling,
          And the wrangling,
        How the danger sinks and swells,
By the sinking or the swelling in the anger of the bells,—
    Of the bells,—
        Of the bells, bells, bells, bells,
          Bells, bells, bells,—
In the clamor and the clanging of the bells!

                    IV

Hear the tolling of the bells,—
          Iron bells!
What a world of solemn thought their monody compels!
    In the silence of the night,
    How they shiver with affright—
Ay, the melancholy menace of their tone!

For every sound that floats
From the rust within their throats
Is a groan.
And the people,—ah, the people,—
They that dwell up in the steeple,
All alone,
And who tolling, tolling, tolling,
In that muffled monotone,
Feel a glory in so rolling
On the human heart a stone,—
They are neither man nor woman,—
They are neither brute nor human,—
They are ghouls:
And their king it is who tolls;
And he rolls, rolls, rolls,
Rolls,
A pæan from the bells!
And his merry bosom swells
With the pæan of the bells!
And he dances and he yells;
Keeping time, time, time,
In a sort of Runic rhyme,
To the pæan of the bells,—
Of the bells:
Keeping time, time, time,
In a sort of Runic rhyme,
To the throbbing of the bells,
Of the bells, bells, bells,—
To the sobbing of the bells;
Keeping time, time, time,
As he knells, knells, knells,

In a happy Runic rhyme,
  To the rolling of the bells,—
    Of the bells, bells, bells,—
  To the tolling of the bells,
    Of the bells, bells, bells, bells,—
      Bells, bells, bells,—
To the moaning and the groaning of the bells.

EDGAR ALLAN POE.

EACH AND ALL

LITTLE thinks, in the field, yon red-cloaked clown
   Of thee from the hill-top looking down;
The heifer that lows in the upland farm,
Far heard, lows not thine ear to charm;
The sexton tolling his bell at noon,
Deems not that great Napoleon
Stops his horse, and lists with delight,
Whilst his files sweep round yon Alpine height;
Nor knowest thou what argument
Thy life to thy neighbor's creed hath lent.
All are needed by each one;
Nothing is fair or good alone.
I thought the sparrow's note from heaven,
Singing at dawn on the alder bough;
I brought him home, in his nest at even;
He sings the song, but it cheers not now,
For I did not bring home the river and sky;
He sang to my ear,—they sang to my eye.
The delicate shells lay on the shore;
The bubbles of the latest wave
Fresh pearls to their enamels gave,
And the bellowing of the savage sea
Greeted their safe escape to me.
I wiped away the weeds and foam,
I fetched my sea-born treasures home;

But the poor, unsightly, noisome things
Had left their beauty on the shore
With the sun and the sand and the wild uproar.
The lover watched his graceful maid,
As 'mid the virgin train she strayed,
Nor knew her beauties best attire
Was woven still by the snow-white choir.
At last she came to his hermitage,
Like the bird from the woodlands to the cage;
The gay enchantment was undone,
A gentle wife, but fairy none.
Then I said, " I covet truth;
Beauty is unripe childhood's cheat;
I leave it behind with the games of youth :"—
As I spoke, beneath my feet
The ground pine curled its pretty wreath,
Running over the club moss burrs;
I inhaled the violet's breath;
Around me stood the oaks and firs;
Pine cones and acorns lay on the ground;
Over me soared the eternal sky,
Full of light and of deity;
Again I saw, again I heard,
The rolling river, the morning bird;
Beauty through all my senses stole;
I yielded myself to the perfect whole.

RALPH WALDO EMERSON

ELEGY WRITTEN IN A COUNTRY CHURCH-YARD

THE curfew tolls the knell of parting day,
  The lowing herds wind slowly o'er the lea,
The ploughman homeward plods his weary way,
  And leaves the world to darkness and to me.

Now fades the glimmering landscape on the sight,
  And all the air a solemn stillness holds,
Save where the beetle wheels his droning flight,
  And drowsy tinklings lull the distant folds;

Save that, from yonder ivy-mantled tower,
  The moping owl does to the moon complain
Of such as, wandering near her secret bower,
  Molest her ancient, solitary reign.

Beneath those rugged elms, that yew-tree's shade,
  Where heaves the turf in many a mould'ring heap,
Each in his narrow cell forever laid,
  The rude forefathers of the hamlet sleep.

The breezy call of incense-breathing morn,
  The swallow twittering from the straw-built shed,
The cock's shrill clarion, or the echoing horn,
  No more shall rouse them from their lowly bed.

For them no more the blazing hearth shall burn,
   Or busy housewife ply her evening care;
No children run to lisp their sire's return,
   Or climb his knees the envied kiss to share.

Oft did the harvest to their sickle yield,
   Their furrow oft the stubborn glebe has broke:
How jocund did they drive their team afield!
   How bowed the woods before their sturdy stroke!

Let not ambition mock their useful toil,
   Their homely joys and destiny obscure;
Nor grandeur hear with a disdainful smile
   The short and simple annals of the poor.

The boast of heraldry, the pomp of power,
   And all that beauty, all that wealth e'er gave,
Await alike th' inevitable hour;
   The paths of glory lead but to the grave.

Nor you, ye proud, impute to these the fault,
   If memory o'er their tombs no trophies raise,
Where, through the long-drawn aisle and fretted vault,
   The pealing anthem swells the note of praise.

Can storied urn, or animated bust,
   Back to its mansion call the fleeting breath?
Can honor's voice provoke the silent dust,
   Or flattery soothe the dull, cold ear of death?

Perhaps in this neglected spot is laid
  Some heart once pregnant with celestial fire;
Hands that the rod of empire might have swayed,
  Or wak'd to ecstasy the living lyre;

But knowledge to their eyes her ample page,
  Rich with the spoils of time, did ne'er unroll;
Chill penury repressed their noble rage,
  And froze the genial current of the soul.

Full many a gem of purest ray serene
  The dark, unfathomed caves of ocean bear:
Full many a flower is born to blush unseen,
  And waste its sweetness on the desert air.

Some village Hampden, that, with dauntless breast,
  The little tyrant of his fields withstood;
Some mute, inglorious Milton here may rest;
  Some Cromwell guiltless of his country's blood.

The applause of list'ning senates to command,
  The threats of pain and ruin to despise,
To scatter plenty o'er a smiling land,
  And read their history in a nation's eyes,

Their lot forbade: nor circumscribed alone
  Their growing virtues, but their crimes confined;
Forbade to wade thro' slaughter to a throne,
  And shut the gates of mercy on mankind;

The struggling pangs of conscious truth to hide,
　To quench the blushes of ingenuous shame,
Or heap the shrine of luxury and pride
　With incense kindled at the Muse's flame.

Far from the madding crowd's ignoble strife,
　Their sober wishes never learned to stray;
Along the cool, sequestered vale of life
　They kept the noiseless tenor of their way.

Yet ev'n these bones from insult to protect,
　Some frail memorial still erected nigh,
With uncouth rhymes and shapeless sculpture deck'd,
　Implores the passing tribute of a sigh.

Their name, their years, spelt by th' unlettered Muse,
　The place of fame and elegy supply;
And many a holy text around she strews,
　That teach the rustic moralist to die.

For who, to dumb forgetfulness a prey,
　This pleasing, anxious being e'er resigned,
Left the warm precincts of the cheerful day,
　Nor cast one longing, lingering look behind?

On some fond breast the parting soul relies,
　Some pious drops the closing eye requires;
E'en from the tomb the voice of Nature cries,
　E'en in our ashes live their wonted fires.

For thee, who mindful of th' unhonor'd dead,
    Dost in these lines their artless tale relate;
If chance, by lonely contemplation led,
    Some kindred spirit shall inquire their fate,—

Haply some hoary-headed swain may say:
    " Oft have we seen him at the peep of dawn,
Brushing with hasty steps the dews away,
    To meet the sun upon the upland lawn.

" There at the foot of yonder nodding beech,
    That wreathes its old fantastic roots so high,
His listless length at noontide would he stretch,
    And pore upon the brook that babbles by.

" Hard by yon wood, now smiling as in scorn,
    Mutt'ring his wayward fancies, he would rove;
Now drooping, woeful-wan, like one forlorn,
    Or craz'd with care, or cross'd in hopeless love.

" One morn I missed him on the custom'd hill,
    Along the heath, and near his favorite tree;
Another came,—nor yet beside the rill,
    Nor up the lawn, nor at the wood was he:

" The next, with dirges due, in sad array,
    Slow through the church-way path we saw him
        borne;—
Approach and read (for thou canst read) the lay
    Grav'd on the stone beneath yon aged thorn."

THE EPITAPH

Here rests his head upon the lap of earth
  A youth, to fortune and to fame unknown;
Fair science frown'd not on his humble birth,
  And melancholy mark'd him for her own.

Large was his bounty, and his soul sincere;
  Heaven did a recompense as largely send:
He gave to misery (all he had) a tear,
  He gained from heaven ('twas all he wished) a friend.

No further seek his merits to disclose,
  Or draw his frailties from their dread abode,—
(There they alike in trembling hope repose,)
  The bosom of his Father and his God.

                                    THOMAS GRAY.

LOCHINVAR

OH, young Lochinvar is come out of the west:
    Through all the wide border his steed was the best
And save his good broadsword he weapons had none,
He rode all unarmed, and he rode all alone.
So faithful in love, and so dauntless in war,
There never was knight like the young Lochinvar.

He stayed not for brake, and he stopped not for stone,
He swam the Eske River where ford there was none;
But, ere he alighted at Netherby gate,
The bride had consented, the gallant came late:
For a laggard in love and a dastard in war
Was to wed the fair Ellen of brave Lochinvar.

So boldly he entered the Netherby hall,
Among bridesmen and kinsmen, and brothers and all.
Then spoke the bride's father, his hand on his sword
(For the poor craven bridegroom said never a word),
" O come ye in peace here, or come ye in war,
Or to dance at our bridal, young Lord Lochinvar? "—

" I long wooed your daughter, my suit you denied;—
Love swells like the Solway, but ebbs like its tide;
And now I am come, with this lost love of mine
To lead but one measure, drink one cup of wine.
There are maidens in Scotland more lovely by far
That would gladly be bride to the young Lochinvar."

The bride kissed the goblet; the knight took it up;
He quaffed off the wine, and he threw down the cup.
She looked down to blush, and she looked up to sigh,
With a smile on her lips and a tear in her eye.
He took her soft hand ere her mother could bar,—
" Now tread me a measure! " said young Lochinvar.

So stately his form, and so lovely her face,
That never a hall such a galliard did grace;
While her mother did fret, and her father did fume,
And the bridegroom stood dangling his bonnet and plume;
And the bride-maidens whispered, " 'Twere better by far
To have matched our fair cousin with young Lochinvar."

One touch to her hand, and one word in her ear,
When they reached the hall door and the charger stood
    near;
So light to the croup the fair lady he swung,
So light to the saddle before her he sprung!
" She is won! we are gone, over bank, bush and scaur!
They'll have fleet steeds that follow! " quoth young
    Lochinvar.

There was mounting 'mong Graemes of the Netherby
    clan;
Forsters, Fenwicks, and Musgraves, they rode and they
    ran;
There was racing and chasing on Cannobie Lee;
But the lost bride of Netherby ne'er did they see.
So daring in love, and so dauntless in war,
Have ye e'er heard of gallant like young Lochinvar?

SIR WALTER SCOTT.

BREATHES THERE THE MAN

BREATHES there the man with soul so dead,
　　Who never to himself hath said,
This is my own, my native land!
Whose heart hath ne'er within him burn'd,
As home his footsteps he hath turn'd
From wandering on a foreign strand!
If such there breathe, go, mark him well;
For him no minstrel raptures swell;
High though his titles, proud his name,
Boundless his wealth as wish can claim,
Despite those titles, power, and pelf,
The wretch, concentred all in self,
Living shall forfeit fair renown,
And, doubly dying, shall go down
To the vile dust from whence he sprung,
Unwept, unhonor'd, and unsung.

SIR WALTER SCOTT.

ON HIS BLINDNESS

WHEN I consider how my light is spent
　　Ere half my days, in this dark world and wide;
And that one talent, which is death to hide,
Lodged with me useless, though my soul more bent
To serve therewith my Maker, and present
My true account, lest he returning chide;
" Doth God exact day-labor, light denied?"
I fondly ask.　But Patience, to prevent
That murmur, soon replies, " God doth not need
Either man's work or his own gifts; who best
Bear his mild yoke, they serve him best: his state
Is kingly; thousands at his bidding speed,
And post o'er land and ocean without rest;
They also serve who only stand and wait."

MILTON.

ON THE RECEIPT OF MY MOTHER'S PICTURE

O THAT those lips had language! Life has passed
    With me but roughly since I heard thee last.
Those lips are thine—thy own sweet smile I see,
The same that oft in childhood solaced me;
Voice only fails, else, how distinct they say,
" Grieve not, my child; chase all thy fears away! "
The meek intelligence of those dear eyes
—Blest be the art that can immortalize,
The art that baffles Time's tyrannic claim
To quench it—here shines on me still the same.
    Faithful remembrancer of one so dear,
O welcome guest, though unexpected here!
Who bid'st me honor with an artless song,
Affectionate, a mother lost so long.
I will obey, not willingly alone,
But gladly, as the precept were her own;
And, while that face renews my filial grief,
Fancy shall weave a charm for my relief,
Shall steep me in Elysian reverie,
A momentary dream, that thou art she.
    My mother! when I learned that thou wast dead,
Say, wast thou conscious of the tears I shed?
Hovered thy spirit o'er thy sorrowing son,

Wretch even then, life's journey just begun?
Perhaps thou gav'st me, though unseen, a kiss;
Perhaps a tear, if souls can weep in bliss—
Ah, that maternal smile! it answers—Yes.
I heard the bell tolled on thy burial day,
I saw the hearse that bore thee slow away,
And, turning from my nursery window, drew
A long, long sigh, and wept a last adieu!
But was it such?—It was.—Where thou art gone,
Adieus and farewells are a sound unknown.
May I but meet thee on that peaceful shore,
The parting word shall pass my lips no more!
The maidens grieved themselves at my concern,
Oft gave me promise of thy quick return.
What ardently I wished, I long believed,
And, disappointed still, was still deceived;
By expectation every day beguiled,
Dupe of to-morrow even from a child.
Thus many a sad to-morrow came and went,
Till, all my stock of infant sorrow spent,
I learned at last submission to my lot,
But, though I less depored thee, ne'er forgot.
    Where once we dwelt our name is heard no more,
Children not thine have trod my nursery floor;
And where the gardener Robin, day by day,
Drew me to school along the public way,
Delighted with my bauble coach and wrapped
In scarlet mantle warm, and velvet cap,
'Tis now become a history little known,
That once we called the pastoral house our own.
Short-lived possession! but the record fair,

That memory keeps of all thy kindness there,
Still outlives many a storm, that has effaced
A thousand other themes less deeply traced.
Thy nightly visits to my chamber made,
That thou might know me safe and warmly laid;
Thy morning bounties, ere I left my home,
The biscuit; or confectionery plum;
The fragrant waters on my cheeks bestowed
By thy own hand, till fresh they shone and glowed;
All this, and more endearing still than all,
Thy constant flow of love that knew no fall.
Ne'er roughened by those cataracts and breaks,
That humor interposed too often makes;
All this still legible in memory's page,
And still to be so to my latest age,
Adds joy to duty, makes me glad to pay
Such honors to thee as my numbers may;
Perhaps a frail memorial, but sincere,
Not scorned in Heaven, though little noticed here.

Could Time, his flight reversed, restore the hours,
When playing with thy vestured tissued flowers,
The violet, the pink, and jessamine,
I pricked them into paper with a pin
—And thou wast happier than myself the while,
Wouldst softly speak, and stroke my head, and smile,—
Could those few pleasant hours again appear,
Might one wish bring them, would I wish them here?
I would not trust my heart—the dear delight
Seems so to be desired, perhaps I might.
But no—what here we call our life is such,
So little to be loved and thou so much,

That I would ill requite thee to constrain
Thy unbound spirit into bonds again.
    Thou, as a gallant bark from Albion's coast
—The storms all weathered and the ocean crossed,—
Shoots into port at some well-havened isle,
Where spices breathe, and brighter seasons smile,
There sits quiescent on the floods, that show
Her beauteous form reflected clear below,
While airs impregnated with incense play
Around her, fanning light her streamers gay;
So thou, with sails how swift! hast reached the shore,
" Where tempests never beat, nor billows roar,"
And thy loved consort on the dangerous tide
Of life long since has anchored by thy side.
But me, scarce hoping to attain that rest,
Always from port withheld, always distressed—
Me howling blasts drive devious, tempest-tossed,
Sails ripped, seams opening wide, and compass lost;
And day by day some current's thwarting force
Sets me more distant from a prosperous course.
But, oh, the thought that thou art safe, and he!
That thought is joy, arrive what may to me.
My boast is not, that I deduce my birth
From loins enthroned, and rulers of the earth;
But higher far my proud pretensions rise—
The son of parents passed into the skies.
And now farewell—Time unrevoked has run
His wonted course, yet what I wished is done.
By contemplation's help, not sought in vain,
I seem to have lived my childhood o'er again;
To have renewed the joys that once were mine,

Without the sin of violating thine;
And, while the wings of Fancy still are free,
And I can view this mimic show of thee,
Time has but half succeeded in his theft—
Thyself removed, thy power to soothe me left.

WILLIAM COWPER.

POLONIUS' ADVICE

[From *Hamlet*.]

YET here, Laertes? aboard, aboard, for shame!
    The wind sits in the shoulder of your sail,
And you are stayed for. There, my blessing with you!
And these few precepts in thy memory
Look thou character. Give thy thoughts no tongue,
Nor any unproportioned thought his act.
Be thou familiar, but by no means vulgar.
The friends thou hast, and their adoption tried,
Grapple them to thy soul with hoops of steel;
But do not dull thy palm with entertainment
Of each new hatch'd, unfledg'd comrade. Beware
Of entrance to a quarrel: but, being in,
Bear't, that the opposed may beware of thee.
Give every man thine ear, but few thy voice:
Take each man's censure, but reserve thy judgment.
Costly thy habit as thy purse can buy,
But not express'd in fancy; rich, not gaudy:
For the apparel oft proclaims the man;
And they in France, of the best rank and station,
Are most select and generous, chief in that.
Neither a borrower nor a lender be:
For loan oft loses both itself and friend;
And borrowing dulls the edge of husbandry.

This above all,—to thine own self be true;
And it must follow, as the night the day,
Thou canst not then be false to any man.
Farewell; my blessing season this in thee!

SHAKESPEARE.

RECESSIONAL

GOD of our fathers, known of old—
   Lord of our far-flung battle line—
Beneath whose awful hand we hold
   Dominion over palm and pine—
Lord God of Hosts, be with us yet,
Lest we forget—lest we forget!

The tumult and the shouting dies—
   The Captains and the Kings depart—
Still stands Thine ancient sacrifice,
   An humble and a contrite heart.
Lord God of Hosts, be with us yet,
Lest we forget—lest we forget!

Far-called, our navies melt away—
   On dune and headland sinks the fire—
Lo, all our pomp of yesterday
   Is one with Nineveh and Tyre!
Judge of the Nations, spare us yet,
Lest we forget—lest we forget!

If, drunk with sight of power, we loose
   Wild tongues that have not Thee in awe—
Such boasting as the Gentiles use,
   Or lesser breeds without the Law—
Lord God of Hosts, be with us yet,
Lest we forget—lest we forget!

For heathen heart that puts her trust
   In reeking tube and iron shard—
All valiant dust that builds on dust,
   And guarding calls not Thee to guard—
For frantic boast and foolish word,
Thy Mercy on Thy People, Lord! *Amen!*

                      RUDYARD KIPLING.

SIR GALAHAD

MY good blade carves the casques of men,
  My tough lance thrusteth sure,
My strength is as the strength of ten,
  Because my heart is pure.
The shattering trumpet shrilleth high,
  The hard brands shiver on the steel,
The splinter'd spear-shafts crack and fly,
  The horse and rider reel:
They reel, they roll in clanging lists,
  And when the tide of combat stands,
Perfume and flowers fall in showers,
  That lightly rain from ladies' hands.

How sweet are looks that ladies bend
  On whom their favors fall!
For them I battle till the end,
  To save from shame and thrall:
But all my heart is drawn above,
  My knees are bowed in crypt and shrine:
I never felt the kiss of love,
  Nor maiden's hand in mine.
More bounteous aspects on me beam,
  Me mightier transports move and thrill;
So keep I fair through faith and prayer
  A virgin heart in work and will.

When down the stormy crescent goes,
  A light before me swims.
Between dark stems the forest glows,
  I hear a noise of hymns:
Then by some secret shrine I ride;
  I hear a voice, but none are there;
The stalls are void, the doors are wide,
  The tapers burning fair.
Fair gleams the snowy altar cloth,
  The silver vessels sparkle clean,
The shrill bell rings, the censer swings,
  And solemn chants resound between.

Sometimes on lonely mountain-meres
  I find a magic bark;
I leap on board; no helmsman steers:
  I float till all is dark.
A gentle sound, an awful light!
  Three angels bear the Holy Grail:
With folded feet, in stoles of white,
  On sleeping wings they sail.
Ah, blessed vision! blood of God!
  My spirit beats her mortal bars,
As down dark tides the glory slides,
  And star-like mingles with the stars.

When on my goodly charger borne
  Through dreaming towns I go,
The cock crows ere the Christmas morn,
  The streets are dumb with snow.

The tempest crackles on the leads,
　And ringing, springs from brand and mail;
But o'er the dark a glory spreads,
　And gilds the driving hail.
I leave the plain, I climb the height;
　No branchy thicket shelter yields;
But blessed forms in whistling storms
　Fly o'er waste fens and windy fields.

A maiden knight—to me is given
　Such hope, I know not fear;
I yearn to breathe the airs of heaven
　That often meet me here.
I muse on you that will not cease,
　Pure spaces clothed in living beams,
Pure lilies of eternal peace,
　Whose odors haunt my dreams;
And, stricken by an angel's hand,
　This mortal armor that I wear,
This weight and size, this heart and eyes,
　Are touched, are turned to finest air.

The clouds are broken in the sky,
　And through the mountain walls
A rolling organ-harmony
　Swells up, and shakes and falls.
Then move the trees, the copses nod,
　Wings flutter, voices hover clear:
" O just and faithful knight of God!
　Ride on! the prize is near."

So pass I hostel, hall and grange;
  By bridge and ford, by park and pale,
All-armed I ride, whate'er betide,
  Until I find the Holy Grail.

                          TENNYSON.

SOUND THE LOUD TIMBREL

SOUND the loud timbrel o'er Egypt's dark sea!
  Jehovah has triumphed,—His people are free!
Sing,—for the pride of the tyrant is broken,
  His chariots, his horsemen, all splendid and brave.
How vain was their boasting!—the Lord hath but spoken,
  And chariots and horsemen are sunk in the wave.
Sound the loud timbrel o'er Egypt's dark sea!
Jehovah has triumphed,—His people are free!

Praise to the Conqueror, praise to the Lord!
His word was our arrow, His breath was our sword!—
Who shall return to tell Egypt the story
  Of those she sent forth in the hour of her pride?
For the Lord hath looked out from His pillar of glory,
  And all her brave thousands are dashed in the tide.
Sound the loud timbrel o'er Egypt's dark sea!
Jehovah has triumphed,—His people are free!

THOMAS MOORE.

ST. AGNES EVE

DEEP on the convent roof the snows
    Are sparkling to the moon:
My breath to heaven like vapor goes:
    May my soul follow soon!
The shadows of the convent towers
    Slant down the snowy sward,
Still creeping with the creeping hours
    That lead me to my Lord:
Make thou my spirit pure and clear
    As are the frosty skies,
Or this first snowdrop of the year
    That in my bosom lies.

As these white robes are soil'd and dark,
    To yonder shining ground,
As this pale taper's earthly spark,
    To yonder argent round;
So shows my soul before the Lamb,
    My spirit before Thee,
So in my earthly house I am,
    To that I hope to be.
Break up the heavens, O Lord! and far,
    Thro' all yon starlight keen,
Draw me, thy bride, a glittering star,
    In raiment white and clean.

He lifts me to the golden doors;
  The flashes come and go;
All heaven bursts her starry floors,
  And strews her lights below,
And deepens on and up! the gates
  Roll back, and far within
For me the Heavenly Bridegroom waits,
  To make me pure of sin.
The sabbaths of eternity,
  One sabbath deep and wide—
A light upon the shining sea—
  The Bridegroom with his bride!

TENNYSON.

THE ANGELS OF BUENA VISTA

SPEAK and tell us, our Ximena, looking northward
    far away,
O'er the camp of the invaders, o'er the Mexican array,
Who is losing? who is winning? are they far or come
    they near?
Look abroad, and tell us, sister, whither rolls the storm
    we hear.

" Down the hills of Angostura still the storm of battle
    rolls;
Blood is flowing, men are dying; God have mercy on
    their souls! "
Who is losing? who is winning?—" Over hill and over
    plain,
I see but smoke of cannon clouding through the mountain
    rain."

Holy Mother! keep our brothers! Look, Ximena, look
    once more.
" Still I see the fearful whirlwind rolling darkly as before,
Bearing on, in strange confusion, friend and foeman, foot
    and horse,
Like some wild and troubled torrent sweeping down its
    mountain course."

Look forth once more, Ximena! "Ah! the smoke has
    rolled away;
And I see the Northern rifles gleaming down the ranks of
    gray.
Hark! that sudden blast of bugles! there the troop of
    Minon wheels;
There the Northern horses thunder, with the cannon at
    their heels.

"Jesu, pity! how it thickens! now retreat and now
    advance!
Right against the blazing cannon shivers Puebla's charg-
    ing lance!
Down they go; the brave young riders; horse and foot
    together fall;
Like a ploughshare in the fallow, through them ploughs
    the Northern ball."

Nearer came the storm and nearer, rolling fast and fright-
    ful on!
Speak, Ximena, speak and tell us, who has lost and who
    has won?
"Alas! alas! I know not; friend and foe together fall,
O'er the dying rush the living: pray, my sisters, for them
    all!

"Lo! the wind the smoke is lifting: Blessed Mother, save
    my brain!
I can see the wounded crawling slowly out from heaps
    of slain.

Now they stagger, blind and bleeding; now they fall and
strive to rise;
Hasten, sisters, haste and save them, lest they die before
our ey s!

" O my heart's love! O my dear one! lay thy poor head
on my knee:
Dost thou know the lips that kiss thee? Canst thou hear
me? canst thou see?
O my husband, brave and gentle! O my Bernal, look
once more
On the blessed cross before thee! Mercy! mercy! all is
o'er! "

Dry thy tears, my poor Ximena; lay thy dear one down
to rest;
Let his hands be meekly folded, lay the cross upon his
breast;
Let his dirge be sung hereafter, and his funeral masses
said:
Today, thou poor bereaved one, the living ask thy aid.

Close beside her, faintly moaning, fair and young, a
soldier lay,
Torn with shot and pierced with lances, bleeding slow
his life away;
But, as tenderly before him the lorn Ximena knelt,
She saw the Northern eagle shining on his pistol-belt.

With a stifled cry of horror straight she turned away her
head;
With a sad and bitter feeling looked she back upon her
dead;
But she heard the youth's low moaning, and his strug-
ling breath of pain,
And she raised the cooling water to his parching lips again.

Whispered low the dying soldier, pressed her hand and
faintly smiled;
Was that pitying face his mother's? did she watch beside
her child?
All his stranger words with meaning her woman's heart
supplied;
With her kiss upon his forehead, " Mother," muttered
he, and died!

" A bitter curse upon them, poor boy, who led thee forth,
From some gentle sad-eyed mother, weeping, lonely, in
the North! "
Spake the mournful Mexic woman, as she laid him with
her dead,
And turned to soothe the living, and bind the wounds
which bled.

Look forth once more, Ximena! " Like a cloud before
the wind
Rolls the battle down the mountains, leaving blood and
death behind;

Ah! they plead in vain for mercy; in the dust the wounded
strive;
Hide your faces, holy angels!   O thou Christ of God,
forgive!"

Sink, O Night, among thy mountains! let the cool gray
shadows fall;
Dying brothers, fighting demons, drop thy curtain over
all!
Through the thickening winter twilight, wide apart the
battle rolled,
In its sheath the sabre rested, and the cannon's lips grew
cold.

But the noble Mexic women still their holy task pursued,
Through that long, dark night of sorrow, worn and faint
and lacking food.
Over weak and suffering brothers, with a tender care
they hung,
And the dying foeman blessed them in a strange and
Northern tongue.

Not wholly lost, O Father! is this evil world of ours;
Upward through its blood and ashes, spring afresh the
Eden flowers;
From its smoking hell of battle, Love and Pity send their
prayer,
And still their white-winged angels hover dimly in our air!

                    JOHN GREENLEAF WHITTIER.

THE AWAKENING OF SPRING

[From *In Memoriam*.]

NOW fades the last long streak of snow,
  Now bourgeons every maze of quick
  About the flowering squares, and thick
By ashen roots the violets blow.

Now rings the woodland loud and long,
  The distance takes a lovelier hue,
  And drowned in yonder living blue
The lark becomes a sightless song.

Now dance the lights on lawn and lea,
  The flocks are whiter down the vale,
  And milkier every milky sail
On winding stream or distant sea;

Where now the seamew pipes, or dives
  In yonder greening gleam, and fly
  The happy birds, that change their sky
To build and brood; that live their lives

From land to land; and in my breast
  Spring wakens, too; and my regret
  Becomes an April violet,
And buds and blossoms like the rest.

                                TENNYSON.

THE BUILDING OF THE SHIP

ALL is finished! and at length
   Has come the bridal day
Of beauty and of strength.
Today the vessel shall be launched!
With fleecy clouds the sky is blanched,
And o'er the bay,
Slowly, in all its splendor dight,
The great sun rises to behold the sight.

   .   .   .   .   .   .

On the deck another bride
Is standing by her lover's side.
Shadows from the flags and shrouds,
Like the shadows cast by clouds,
Broken by many a sunny fleck,
Fall around them on the deck.

   .   .   .   .   ◆   .

Then the Master,
With a gesture of command,
Waved his hand;
And at the word,
Loud and sudden there was heard,
All around them and below,
The sound of hammers, blow on blow,
Knocking away the shores and spurs.
And see! she stirs!

She starts,—she moves, she seems to feel
The thrill of life along her keel,
And spurning with her foot the ground,
With one exulting, joyous bound,
She leaps into the ocean's arms!

     .   .   .   o   .   .

Sail forth into the sea of life,
O gentle, loving, trusting wife,
And safe from all adversity
Upon the bosom of that sea
Thy comings and thy goings be!
For gentleness and love and trust
Prevail o'er angry wave and gust;
And in the wreck of noble lives
Something immortal still survives!

Thou, too, sail on, O Ship of State!
Sail on, O Union, strong and great!
Humanity with all its fears,
With all the hopes of future years,
Is hanging breathless on thy fate!
We know what Master laid thy keel,
What Workman wrought thy ribs of steel,
Who made each mast, and sail, and rope,
What anvils rang, what hammers beat,
In what a forge and what a heat
Were shaped the anchors of thy hope!
Fear not each sudden sound and shock,
'Tis of the wave, and not the rock;
'Tis but the flapping of the sail,
And not a rent made by the gale!

In spite of rock and tempest's roar,
In spite of false lights on the shore,
Sail on, nor fear to breast the sea!
Our hearts, our hopes, are all with thee,
Our hearts, our hopes, our prayers, our tears,
Our faith triumphant o'er our fears,
Are all with thee,—are all with thee!

LONGFELLOW.

THE CHAMBERED NAUTILUS

THIS is the ship of pearl, which, poets feign,
    Sails the unshadowed main,—
The venturous bark that flings
On the sweet summer wind its purpled wings
In gulfs enchanted, where the Siren sings,
And coral reefs lie bare,
Where the cold sea-maids rise to sun their streaming hair.

Its webs of living gauze no more unfurl;
Wrecked is the ship of pearl!
And every chambered cell,
Where its dim dreaming life was wont to dwell,
As the frail tenant shaped his growing shell,
Before thee lies revealed,—
Its irised ceiling rent, its sunless crypt unsealed!

Year after year beheld the silent toil
That spread its lustrous coil;
Still as the spiral grew,
He left the past year's dwelling for the new,
Stole with soft step his shining archway through,
Built up its idle door,
Stretched in his last found home, and knew the old no
    more.

Thanks for the heavenly message brought by thee,
Child of the wandering sea,
Cast from her lap, forlorn!
From thy dead lips a clearer note is born
Than ever Triton blew from wreath'd horn!
While on mine ear it rings,
Through the deep caves of thought I hear a voice that
    sings:

Build thee more stately mansions, O my soul,
As the swift seasons roll!
Leave thy low-vaulted past!
Let each new temple, nobler than the last,
Shut thee from heaven with a dome more vast,
Till thou at length art free,
Leaving thine outgrown shell by life's unresting sea!
                              OLIVER WENDELL HOLMES.

THE CLOUD

I BRING fresh showers for the thirsting flowers,
   From the seas and the streams;
I bear light shades for the leaves when laid
   In their noonday dreams.
From my wings are shaken the dews that waken
   The sweet buds every one,
When rocked to rest on their mother's breast,
   As she dances about the sun.
I wield the flail of the lashing hail,
   And whiten the green plains under;
And then again I dissolve it in rain,
   And laugh as I pass in thunder.

    .   .   .   .   .   .

I sift the snow on the mountain below,
   And their great pines groan aghast;
And all the night 'tis my pillow white,
   While I sleep in the arms of the blast.
Sublime on the towers of my skyey bowers,
   Lightning, my pilot, sits;
In a cavern under is fettered the thunder,
   It struggles and howls at fits;
Over earth and ocean, with gentle motion,
   This pilot is guiding me,
Lured by the love of the genii that move
   In the depths of the purple sea;

Over the rills, and the crags, and the hills,
  Over the lakes and the plains,
Wherever he dream, under mountain or stream,
  The spirit he loves remains;
And I all the while bask in heaven's blue smile,
  Whilst he is dissolving in rains.

PERCY BYSSHE SHELLEY.

THE LAST LEAF

I SAW him once before,
  As he passed by the door,
    And again
The pavement stones resound
As he totters o'er the ground,
    With his cane.

They say that in his prime,
Ere the pruning knife of Time
    Cut him down,
Not a better man was found
By the crier on his round
    Through the town.

But now he walks the streets,
And he looks at all he meets,
    Sad and wan,
And he shakes his feeble head,
And it seems as if he said:
    "They are gone!"

The mossy marbles rest
On the lips that he has pressed
    In their bloom;
And the names he loved to hear
Have been carved for many a year
    On the tomb.

My grandmamma has said—
Poor old lady! she is dead
    Long ago—
That he had a Roman nose,
And his cheek was like a rose
    In the snow.

But now his nose is thin,
And it rests upon his chin
    Like a staff;
And a crook is in his back,
And a melancholy crack
    In his laugh.

I know it is a sin
For me to sit and grin
    At him here;
But the old three-cornered hat,
And the breeches, and all that,
    Are so queer!

And if I should live to be
The last leaf upon the tree
    In the spring,
Let them smile, as I do now,
At the old forsaken bough
    Where I cling.

             OLIVER WENDELL HOLMES.

THE RAINBOW

MY heart leaps up when I behold
    A rainbow in the sky;
So was it when my life began,
So is it now I am a man,
So be it when I shall grow old,
        Or let me die!
The Child is father of the Man;
And I could wish my days to be
Bound each to each by natural piety.

WORDSWORTH.

THE ROYAL GEORGE

TOLL for the brave!
  The brave that are no more!
All sunk beneath the wave,
  Fast by their native shore!

Eight hundred of the brave,
  Whose courage well was tried,
Had made the vessel heel,
  And laid her on her side.

A land breeze shook the shrouds,
  And she was overset;
Down went the Royal George
  With all her crew complete.

Toll for the brave!
  Brave Kempenfelt is gone;
His last sea fight is fought,
  His work of glory done.

It was not in the battle;
  No tempest gave the shock;
She sprang no fatal leak,
  She ran upon no rock.

His sword was in its sheath,
  His fingers held the pen,
When Kempenfelt went down
  With twice four hundred men.

Weigh the vessel up,
  Once dreaded by our foes!
And mingle with our cup
  The tear that England owes.

Her timbers yet are sound
  And she may float again
Full charged with England's thunder,
  And plough the distant main.

But Kempenfelt is gone,
  His victories are o'er;
And he and his eight hundred
  Shall plough the wave no more.

                    WILLIAM COWPER.

TO A SKYLARK

HAIL to thee, blithe spirit!
  Bird thou never wert,
That from heaven, or near it,
  Pourest thy full heart
In profuse strains of unpremeditated art.

  Higher still and higher
    From the earth thou springest,
  Like a cloud of fire;
    The blue deep thou wingest,
And singing still dost soar, and soaring ever singest.

  In the golden lightning
    Of the setting sun,
  O'er which clouds are brightening,
    Thou dost float and run;
Like an unbodied joy whose race is just begun.

  The pale purple even
    Melts around thy flight;
  Like a star of heaven,
    In the broad daylight
Thou art unseen, but yet I hear thy shrill delight.

TO A SKYLARK

Keen as are the arrows
  Of the silver sphere,
Whose intense lamp narrows
  In the white dawn clear,
Until we hardly see, we feel that it is there.

All the earth and air
  With thy voice is loud,
As, when night is bare,
  From one lonely cloud
The moon rains out her beams, and heaven is overflowed.

What thou art we know not;
  What is most like thee?
From rainbow clouds there flow not
  Drops so bright to see,
As from thy presence showers a rain of melody.

Like a poet hidden
  In the light of thought,
Singing hymns unbidden,
  Till the world is wrought
To sympathy with hopes and fears it heeded not:

Like a high-born maiden
  In a palace-tower,
Soothing her love-laden
  Soul in secret hour
With music sweet as love, which overflows her bower:

Like a glow-worm golden,
   In a dell of dew,
Scattering unbeholden
   Its aerial hue
Among the flowers and grass which screen it from the
   view:

Like a rose embowered
   In its own green leaves,
By warm winds deflowered,
   Till the scent it gives
Makes faint with too much sweet these heavy wingèd
   thieves.

Sound of vernal showers
   On the twinkling grass,
Rain-awakened flowers,
   All that ever was
Joyous and clear and fresh thy music doth surpass.

Teach us, sprite or bird,
   What sweet thoughts are thine:
I had never heard
   Praise of love or wine
That panted forth a flood of rapture so divine.

Chorus hymeneal,
   Or triumphant chaunt,
Matched with thine, would be all
   But an empty vaunt,—
A thing wherein we feel there is some hidden want.

What objects are fountains
    Of thy happy strain?
What fields, or waves, or mountains?
    What shapes of sky or plain?
What love of thine own kind? what ignorance of pain?

With thy clear, keen joyance
    Languor cannot be;
Shades of annoyance
    Never came to thee:
Thou lovest, but ne'er knew love's sad satiety.

Waking or asleep,
    Thou of death must deem
Things more true and deep
    Than we mortals dream,
Or how could thy notes flow in such crystal stream?

We look before and after,
    And pine for what is not:
Our sincerest laughter
    With some pain is fraught;
Our sweetest songs are those that tell of saddest thought.

Yet if we could scorn
    Hate and pride and fear,
If we were things born
    Not to shed a tear,
I know not how thy joy we ever should come near.

Better than all measures
Of delightful sound,
Better than all treasures
That in books are found,
Thy skill to poet were, thou scorner of the ground!

Teach me half the gladness
That thy brain must know,
Such harmonious madness
From thy lips would flow,
The world should listen then, as I am listening now.

PERCY BYSSHE SHELLEY.

WATERLOO

[From *Childe Harold's Pilgrimage.*]

THERE was a sound of revelry by night,
   And Belgium's capital had gather'd then
Her beauty and her chivalry, and bright
    The lamps shone o'er fair women and brave men·
    A thousand hearts beat happily; and when
Music arose with its voluptuous swell,
    Soft eyes look'd love to eyes that spake again,
And all went merry as a marriage bell;
But hush! hark! a rising sound strikes like a rising knell!

Did ye not hear it?—No; 'twas but the wind,
   Or the car rattling o'er the stony street;
On with the dance! let joy be unconfined;
    No sleep till morn, when Youth and Pleasure meet
    To chase the glowing hours with flying feet.—
But hark!—that heavy sound breaks in once more,
    As if the clouds its echoes would repeat;
And nearer, clearer, deadlier than before!
Arm! arm! it is—it is—the cannon's opening roar!

Within a windowed niche of that high hall
   Sate Brunswick's fated chieftain; he did hear
That sound, the first amid the festival,
    And caught its tone with Death's prophetic ear;
    And when they smiled because he deemed it near,

His heart more truly knew that peal too well
  Which stretched his father on a bloody bier,
And roused the vengeance blood alone could quell:
He rush'd into the field, and foremost fighting fell.

Ah! then and there was hurrying to and fro,
  And gathering tears and tremblings of distress,
And cheeks all pale, which but an hour ago
  Blush'd at the praise of their own loveliness;
  And there were sudden partings, such as press
The life from out young hearts, and choking sighs
  Which ne'er might be repeated: who could guess
If ever more should meet those mutual eyes,
Since upon nights so sweet such awful morn could rise!

And there was mounting in hot haste: the steed,
  The mustering squadron, and the clattering car,
Went pouring forward with impetuous speed,
  And swiftly forming in the ranks of war;
  And the deep thunder peal on peal afar;
And near, the beat of the alarming drum
  Roused up the soldier e'er the morning star;
While throng'd the citizens with terror dumb,
Or whispering with white lips—" The foe! They come!
      They come! "

And wild and high the " Cameron's Gathering " rose!
  The war-note of Lochiel, which Albyn's hills
Have heard, and heard, too, have her Saxon foes:—
  How in the noon of night that pibroch thrills
  Savage and shrill! But with the breath which fills

Their mountain pipe, so fill the mountaineers
  With the fierce native daring which instils
The stirring memory of a thousand years,
And Evan's, Donald's fame rings in each clansman's ears!

And Ardennes waves above them her green leaves,
  Dewy with Nature's teardrops, as they pass,
Grieving, if aught inanimate e'er grieves,
  Over the unreturning brave,—alas!
  Ere evening to be trodden like the grass
Which now beneath them, but above shall grow
  In its next verdure, when this fiery mass
Of living vapor, rolling on the foe,
And burning with high hope, shall moulder cold and low.

Last noon beheld them full of lusty life,
  Last eve in beauty's circle proudly gay,
The midnight brought the signal sound of strife,
  The morn the marshalling in arms,—the day
  Battle's magnificently stern array!
The thunder-clouds close o'er it, which when rent
  The earth is covered thick with other clay,
Which her own clay shall cover, heaped and pent,
Rider and horse,—friend, foe,—in one red burial blent!

LORD BYRON.

PATRIOTIC

FOR ALL GRADES

HAIL! COLUMBIA

HAIL! Columbia, happy land!
Hail! ye heroes, heaven-born band!
Who fought and bled in freedom's cause,
Who fought and bled in freedom's cause,
And when the storm of war was gone
Enjoyed the peace your valor won.
Let independence be our boast,
Ever mindful what it cost;
Ever grateful for the prize;
Let its altar reach the skies.

Firm united let us be,
Rallying round our liberty.
As a band of brothers joined,
Peace and safety we shall find.

Immortal patriots, rise once more,
Defend your rights, defend your shore,
Let no rude foe with impious hand,
Let no rude foe with impious hand,
Invade the shrine where sacred lies
Of toil and blood the well-earned prize!
While off'ring peace sincere and just
In heaven we place a manly trust
That truth and justice shall prevail
And every scheme of bondage fail.

CHORUS.

Sound, sound the trump of fame!
Let our own Washington's great name
Ring through the world with loud applause;
Ring through the world with loud applause;
Let ev'ry clime to freedom dear,
Listen with a joyful ear.
With equal skill, with godlike power
He governs in the fearful hour
Of horrid war, or guides with ease
The happier times of honest peace.

CHORUS.

Behold the chief who now commands,
Once more, to serve his country, stands,
The rock on which the storm will beat.
The rock on which the storm will beat.
But, sound in virtue, firm and true,
His hopes are fixed on heaven and you.
When hope was sinking in dismay,
When glooms obscured Columbia's day,
His steady mind, from charges free,
Resolved on death or liberty.

CHORUS.

JOSEPH HOPKINSON.

THE AMERICAN FLAG

WHEN freedom from her mountain height,
    Unfurled her standard to the air,
She tore the azure robe of night,
And set the stars of glory there!
She mingled with its gorgeous dyes
The milky baldric of the skies,
And striped its pure, celestial white
With streakings of the morning light;
Then, from his mansion in the sun,
She called her eagle bearer down,
And gave into his mighty hand
The symbol of her chosen land!

Majestic monarch of the cloud!
Who rear'st aloft thy regal form,
To hear the tempest trumpings loud,
And see the lightning lances driven,
When strive the warriors of the storm,
And rolls the thunder drum of heaven!—
Child of the Sun! to thee 'tis given
To guard the banner of the free,
To hover in the sulphur smoke,
To ward away the battle stroke,
And bid its blendings shine afar,
Like rainbows on the cloud of war,
The harbingers of victory!

Flag of the brave! thy folds shall fly,
The sign of hope and triumph high!
When speaks the signal trumpet tone,
And the long line comes gleaming on,
Ere yet the life blood, warm and wet,
Has dimmed the glistening bayonet,
Each soldier's eye shall brightly turn
To where the sky-born glories burn,
And, as his springing steps advance,
Catch war and vengeance from the glance.
And when the cannon's mouthings loud
Heave in wild wreaths the battle shroud,
And gory sabres rise and fall
Like shoots of flame on midnight's pall;
Then shall thy meteor glances glow,
And cowering foes shall shrink below
Each gallant arm that strikes beneath
That lovely messenger of death.

Flag of the seas! on ocean's wave
Thy stars shall glitter o'er the brave;
When death, careering on the gale,
Sweeps darkly round the bellied sail,
And frightened waves rush wildly back
Before the broadside's reeling rack,
Each dying wandering of the sea
Shall look at once to heaven and thee,
And smile to see thy splendors fly
In triumph o'er his closing eye.

Flag of the free heart's hope and home!
By angel hands to valor given,
Thy stars have lit the welkin dome,
And all thy hues were born in heaven.
Forever float that standard sheet!
Where breathes the foe that falls before us,
With Freedom's soil beneath our feet,
And Freedom's banner streaming o'er us?

JOSEPH RODMAN DRAKE.

A SONG OF THE CAMP

"GIVE us a song!" the soldiers cried,
    The outer trenches guarding,
When the heated guns of the camps allied
    Grew weary of bombarding.

The dark Redan, in silent scoff,
    Lay, grim and threatening, under;
And the tawny mound of the Malakoff
    No longer belched its thunder.

There was a pause. A guardsman said:
    "We storm the forts to-morrow;
Sing while we may, another day
    Will bring enough of sorrow."

They lay along the battery's side
    Below the smoking cannon;
Brave hearts from Severn and from Clyde
    And from the banks of Shannon.

They sang of love and not of fame,
    Forgot was Britain's glory,
Each heart recalled a different name,
    But all sang "Annie Laurie."

Voice after voice caught up the song
   Until its tender passion
Rose like an anthem rich and strong—
   Their battle-eve confession.

Dear girl, her name he dared not speak,
   But as the song grew louder,
Something upon the soldier's cheek
   Washed off the stains of powder.

Beyond the darkening ocean burned
   The bloody sunset's embers,
While the Crimean valleys learned
   How English love remembers.

And once again a fire of Hell
   Rained on the Russian quarters,
With scream of shot and burst of shell
   And bellowing of the mortars!

And Irish Nora's eyes are dim
   For the singer dumb and gory;
And English Mary mourns for him
   Who sang of " Annie Laurie."

Sleep, soldiers! still in honored rest,
   Your truth and valor wearing;
The bravest are the tenderest—
   The loving are the daring.
                            BAYARD TAYLOR.

BARBARA FRIETCHIE

UP from the meadows rich with corn,
   Clear in the cool September morn,

The clustered spires of Frederick stand
Green-walled by the hills of Maryland.

Round about them orchards sweep,
Apple and peach tree fruited deep,

Fair as the garden of the Lord
To the eyes of the famished rebel horde;

On that pleasant morn of the early fall
When Lee marched over the mountain wall,—

Over the mountains, winding down,
Horse and foot into Frederick town.

Forty flags with their silver stars,
Forty flags with their crimson bars,

Flapped in the morning wind; the sun
Of noon looked down, and saw not one.

Up rose old Barbara Frietchie then,
Bowed with her four-score years and ten;

Bravest of all in Frederick town
She took up the flag the men hauled down;

In her attic window the staff she set,
To show that one heart was loyal yet.

Up the street came the rebel tread,
Stonewall Jackson riding ahead.

Under his slouch hat, left and right,
He glanced: the old flag met his sight.

" Halt! "—the dust-browned ranks stood fast;
" Fire! " out blazed the rifle blast.

It shivered the window, pane and sash;
It rent the banner with seam and gash.

Quick, as it fell from the broken staff
Dame Barbara snatched the silken scarf;

She leaned far out on the window sill,
And shook it forth with a royal will.

" Shoot, if you must, this old gray head,
But spare your country's flag," she said.

A shade of sadness, a blush of shame,
Over the face of the leader came;

The nobler nature within him stirred
To life at that woman's deed and word:

"Who touches a hair of yon gray head
Dies like a dog! March on!" he said.

All day long through Frederick street
Sounded the tread of marching feet;

All day long that free flag tost
Over the heads of the rebel host.

Ever its torn folds rose and fell
On the loyal winds that loved it well;

And through the hill-gaps sunset light
Shone over it with a warm good-night.

Barbara Frietchie's work is o'er,
And the rebel rides on his raids no more.

Honor to her! and let a tear
Fall, for her sake, on Stonewall's bier.

Over Barbara Frietchie's grave
Flag of freedom and union, wave!

Peace and order and beauty draw
Round thy symbol of light and law;

And ever the stars above look down
On thy stars below in Frederick town!

JOHN GREENLEAF WHITTIER.

CONCORD HYMN

BY the rude bridge that arched the flood,
   Their flag to April's breeze unfurled,
Here once the embattled farmers stood,
   And fired the shot heard round the world.

The foe long since in silence slept;
   Alike the conqueror silent sleeps;
And Time the ruined bridge has swept
   Down the dark stream which seaward creeps.

On this green bank, by this soft stream,
   We set today a votive stone;
That memory may their deed redeem,
   When, like our sires, our sons are gone.

Spirit, that made those spirits dare
   To die, and leave their children free,
Bid Time and Nature gently spare
   The shaft we raise to them and thee.

                    RALPH WALDO EMERSON.

NATHAN HALE

TO drum beat and heart beat
   A soldier marches by;
There is color in his cheek,
   There is courage in his eye;
Yet to drum beat and heart beat
   In a moment he must die.

By starlight and moonlight
   He seeks the Briton's camp,
And he hears the rustling flag
   And the armèd sentry's tramp,
And the starlight and the moonlight
   His silent wanderings lamp.

With slow tread and still tread
   He scans the tented line;
And he counts the battery guns
   By the gaunt and shadowy pine;
And his slow tread and still tread
   Gives no warning sign.

The dark wave, the plumed wave,
   It meets his eager glance;
And it sparkles 'neath the stars
   Like the glimmer of a lance;

A dark wave, a plumed wave,
  On an emerald expanse.

A sharp clang, a steel clang,
  And terror in the sound!
For the sentry, falcon-eyed,
  In the camp a spy hath found;
With a sharp clang, a steel clang,
  The patriot is bound.

With calm brow, steady brow,
  He robes him for the tomb;
In his look there is no fear,
Nor a shadow trace of gloom;
But with calm brow, and steady brow,
  He robes him for the tomb.

Through the long night, the still night,
  He kneels upon the sod,
And the brutal guards withhold
  E'en the solemn word of God!
Through the long night, the still night,
  He walks where Christ hath trod.

In the blue morn, the sunny morn,
  He dies upon the tree,
And mourns that he can lose
  But one life for liberty;
In the blue morn, the sunny morn,
  His spirit wings are free.

But his last words, his message words,
  They burn, lest friendly eye
Should read how proud and calm
  A patriot could die,
With his last words, his message words,
  A soldier's battle-cry.

From Fame-leaf and Angel-leaf,
  From monument and urn,
The sad of earth, the glad of heaven,
  His tragic fate shall learn;
And on Fame-leaf and Angel-leaf,
  The name of Hale shall burn.

                              FRANCIS M. FINCH

OLD IRONSIDES

AY, tear her tattered ensign down!
 Long has it waved on high,
And many an eye has danced to see
 That banner in the sky;
Beneath it rung the battle shout,
 And burst the cannon's roar;—
The meteor of the ocean air
 Shall sweep the clouds no more.

Her deck, once red with heroes' blood,
 Where knelt the vanquished foe,
When winds were hurrying o'er the flood,
 And waves were white below,
No more shall feel the victor's tread,
 Or know the conquered knee;
The harpies of the shore shall pluck
 The eagle of the sea!

Oh, better that her shattered hulk
 Should sink beneath the wave;
Her thunders shook the mighty deep,
 And there should be her grave:
Nail to the mast her holy flag,
 Set every threadbare sail,
And give her to the gods of storms,
 The lightning and the gale!

                    OLIVER WENDELL HOLMES.

SOLDIER, REST!

[Song from *The Lady of the Lake*.]

SOLDIER, rest! thy warfare o'er,
 Sleep the sleep that knows not breaking;
Dream of battle-fields no more,
 Days of danger, nights of waking.
In our isle's enchanted hall,
 Hands unseen thy couch are strewing;
Fairy strains of music fall,
 Every sense in slumber dewing.
Soldier, rest! thy warfare o'er,
Dream of fighting fields no more;
Sleep the sleep that knows not breaking,
Morn of toil, nor night of waking.

No rude sound shall reach thine ear,
 Armor's clang, or war-steed champing,
Trump nor pibroch summon here,
 Mustering clan, or squadron tramping,
Yet the lark's shrill fife may come,
 At the daybreak, from the fallow,
And the bittern sound his drum,
 Booming from the sedgy shallow.
Ruder sounds shall none be near,
Guard's nor warder's challenge here;
Here's no war-steed's neigh and champing,
Shouting clans, or squadrons stamping.

Huntsman, rest! thy chase is done,
  While our slumberous spells assail ye,
Dream not, with the rising sun,
  Bugles here shall sound reveillè.
Sleep! the deer is in his den;
  Sleep! thy hounds are by thee lying;
Sleep! nor dream, in yonder glen,
  How thy gallant steed lay dying.
Huntsman, rest! thy chase is done,
Think not of the rising sun,
For at dawning to assail ye,
Here no bugles sound reveillè.

                        WALTER SCOTT.

SONG OF MARION'S MEN

OUR band is few, but true and tried,
　　Our leader frank and bold;
The British soldier trembles
　　When Marion's name is told.
Our fortress is the good greenwood,
　　Our tent the cypress tree;
We know the forest round us,
　　As seamen know the sea;
We know its walls of thorny vines,
　　Its glades of reedy grass,
Its safe and silent islands
　　Within the dark morass.

Woe to the English soldiery
　　That little dread us near!
On them shall light at midnight
　　A strange and sudden fear;
When, waking to their tents on fire,
　　They grasp their arms in vain,
And they who stand to face us
　　Are beat to earth again;
And they who fly in terror deem
　　A mighty host behind,
And hear the tramp of thousands
　　Upon the hollow wind.

Then sweet the hour that brings release
  From danger and from toil;
We talk the battle over,
  And share the battle's spoil.
The woodland rings with laugh and shout,
  As if a hunt were up,
And woodland flowers are gathered
  To crown the soldier's cup.
With merry songs we mock the wind
  That in the pine-tops grieves,
And slumber long and sweetly
  On beds of oaken leaves.

Well knows the fair and friendly moon
  The band that Marion leads,—
The glitter of their rifles,
  The scampering of their steeds.
'Tis life to guide the fiery barb
  Across the moonlight plain;
'Tis life to feel the night-wind
  That lifts his tossing mane.
A moment in the British camp—
  A moment—and away
Back to the pathless forest
  Before the peep of day.

Grave men there are by broad Santee,
  Grave men with hoary hairs;
Their hearts are all with Marion,
  For Marion are their prayers.

And lovely ladies greet our band
  With kindliest welcoming,
With smiles like those of summer,
  And tears like those of spring.
For them we wear these trusty arms,
  And lay them down no more
Till we have driven the Briton
  Forever from our shore.

WILLIAM CULLEN BRYANT.

THE BLUE AND THE GRAY

BY the flow of the inland river,
  Whence the fleets of iron have fled,
Where the blades of grave grass quiver,
  Asleep are the ranks of the dead;
Under the sod and the dew,
  Waiting the judgment day—
Under the one, the blue;
  Under the other, the gray.

These in the robings of glory,
  Those in the gloom of defeat,
All, with the battle blood gory,
  In the dusk of eternity meet;
Under the sod and the dew,
  Waiting the judgment day—
Under the laurel, the blue;
  Under the willow, the gray.

From the silence of sorrowful hours
  The desolate mourners go,
Lovingly laden with flowers
  Alike for the friend and the foe;
Under the sod and the dew,
  Waiting the judgment day—
Under the roses, the blue;
  Under the lilies, the gray.

So with an equal splendor
    The morning sun-rays fall,
With a touch impartially tender,
    On the blossoms blooming for all;
Under the sod and the dew,
    Waiting the judgment day—
'Broidered with gold, the blue;
    Mellowed with gold, the gray.

So when the summer calleth
    On forest and field of grain,
With an equal murmur falleth
    The cooling drip of the rain;
Under the sod and the dew,
    Waiting the judgment day—
Wet with rain, the blue;
    Wet with rain, the gray.

Sadly, but not with upbraiding,
    The generous deed was done;
In the storm of the years that are fading,
    No braver battle was won;
Under the sod and the dew,
    Waiting the judgment day—
Under the blossoms, the blue;
    Under the garlands, the gray.

No more shall the war-cry sever,
    Or the winding rivers be red;
They banish our anger forever
    When they laurel the graves of our dead!

Under the sod and the dew,
  Waiting the judgment day—
Love and tears for the blue;
  Tears and love for the gray.

FRANCIS M. FINCH.

THE RISING IN 1776

OUT of the North the wild news came,
    Far flashing on the wings of flame,
Swift as the boreal light which flies
At midnight through the startled skies.
And there was tumult in the air,
The fife's shrill note, the drum's loud beat,
And through the wide land everywhere
The answering tread of hurrying feet;
While the first oath of Freedom's gun
Came of the blast from Lexington;
And Concord roused, no longer tame,
Forgot her old baptismal name,
Made bare her patriot arm of power,
And swelled the discord of the hour.

    .   .   .   .   .   .

Within its shade of elm and oak
The church of Berkley Manor stood;
There Sunday found the rural folk,
And some esteemed of gentle blood.
In vain their feet with loitering tread
Passed 'mid the graves where rank is naught;
All could not read the lesson taught
In that republic of the dead.

How sweet the hour of Sabbath talk,
The vale with peace and sunshine full,
Where all the happy people walk,
Decked in their homespun flax and wool!
Where youth's gay hats with blossoms bloom;
And every maid, with simple art,
Wears on her breast, like her own heart,
A bud whose depths are all perfume;
While every garment's gentle stir
Is breathing rose and lavender.

.   .   .   .   .   .

The pastor came: his snowy locks
Hallowed his brow of thought and care;
And calmly, as shepherds lead their flocks,
He led into the house of prayer.
The pastor rose; the prayer was strong;
The psalm was warrior David's song;
The text, a few short words of might,—
" The Lord of Hosts shall arm the right!"

He spoke of wrongs too long endured,
Of sacred rights to be secured;
Then from his patriot tongue of flame
The startling words for freedom came.
The stirring sentences he spake
Compelled the heart to glow or quake,
And, rising on his theme's broad wing,
And grasping in his nervous hand
The imaginary battle brand,
In face of death he dared to fling
Defiance to a tyrant king.

Even as he spoke, his frame, renewed,
In eloquence of attitude,
Rose, as it seemed, a shoulder higher;
Then swept his kindling glance of fire
From startled pew to breathless choir;
When suddenly his mantle wide
His hands impatient flung aside,
And lo! he met their wondering eyes
Complete in all a warrior's guise.

A moment there was awful pause,—
When Berkley cried, " Cease, traitor! cease!
God's temple is the house of peace! "
The other shouted, " Nay, not so,
When God is with his righteous cause;
His holiest places then are ours,
His temples are our forts and towers
That frown upon the tyrant foe;
In this the dawn of Freedom's day
There is a time to fight and pray! "

And now before the open door—
The warrior-priest had ordered so—
The enlisting trumpet's sudden roar
Rang through the chapel, o'er and o'er,
Its long reverberating blow,
So loud and clear, it seemed the ear
Of dusty death must wake and hear.
And there the startling drum and fife
Fired the living with fiercer life;

While overhead, with wild increase,
Forgetting its ancient toll of peace,
The great bell swung as ne'er before.
It seemed as it would never cease;
And every word its ardor flung
From off its jubilant iron tongue
Was " War! War! War!"

" Who dares "—this was the patriot's cry,
As striding from the desk he came,—
" Come out with me, in Freedom's name,
For her to live, for her to die?"
A hundred hands flung up reply,
A hundred voices answered, " I."

T. Buchanan Read.

THE STAR-SPANGLED BANNER

O SAY can you see, by the dawn's early light,
   What so proudly we hailed at the twilight's last
      gleaming?
Whose broad stripes and bright stars, through the perilous
      fight,
   O'er the ramparts we watched were so gallantly stream-
      ing?
And the rockets' red glare, the bombs bursting in air,
Gave proof through the night that our flag was still there;
O! does that star-spangled banner yet wave
O'er the land of the free and the home of the brave?

On the shore, dimly seen through the mists of the deep,
   Where the foe's haughty host in dread silence reposes,
What is that which the breeze, o'er the towering steep,
   As it fitfully blows, half conceals, half discloses?
Now it catches the gleam of the morning's first beam;
Its full glory reflected now shines on the stream:
'Tis the star-spangled banner; O! long may it wave
O'er the land of the free and the home of the brave.

And where is the band who so vauntingly swore,
   'Mid the havoc of war and the battle's confusion,
A home and a country they'd leave us no more,
   Their blood hath washed out their foul footstep's pollu-
      tion;

No refuge could save the hireling and slave
From the terror of flight and the gloom of the grave;
And the star-spangled banner in triumph doth wave
O'er the land of the free and the home of the brave.

O! thus be it ever when freemen shall stand
    Between our loved home and the war's desolation;
Bless'd with peace, may the heaven-rescued land
    Praise the Power that hath made and preserved us a
        nation!
Then conquer we must, when our cause it is just,
And this be our motto, " In God is our trust ";
And the star-spangled banner in triumph shall wave
O'er the land of the free and the home of the brave.

FRANCIS SCOTT KEY.

WAR-SONG

FREEDOM calls you! Quick! be ready,—
  Rouse ye in the name of God!
Onward, onward! strong and steady,—
  Dash to earth the oppressor's rod.
Freedom calls, ye brave, ye brave!
Rise, and spurn the name of slave.

Grasp the sword!—its edge is keen;
  Seize the gun! its ball is true:
Sweep your land from tyrant clean,—
  Haste, and scour it through and through!
Onward, onward! Freedom cries;
Rush to arms,—the tyrant flies.

Freedom calls you! Quick! be ready,—
  Think of what your sires have been.
Onward, onward! strong and steady,—
  Drive the tyrant to his den!
On! and let the watchwords be,
Country, home, and liberty!

JAMES G. PERCIVAL

WARREN'S ADDRESS

STAND! the ground's your own, my braves!
   Will ye give it up to slaves?
Will ye look for greener graves?
   Hope ye mercy still?
What's the mercy despots feel?
Hear it in that battle peal!
Read it on yon bristling steel!
   Ask it, ye who will!

Fear ye foes who kill for hire?
Will ye to your homes retire?
Look behind you! they're a-fire!
   And, before you, see
Who have done it! From the vale
On they come! and will ye quail?
Leaden rain and leaden hail
   Let their welcome be!

In the God of battles trust!
Die we may, and die we must;
But oh, where can dust to dust
   Be consigned so well,
As where heaven its dews shall shed
On the martyred patriot's bed,
And the rocks shall raise their head,
   Of his deeds to tell!

JOHN PIERPONT.

QUOTATIONS

MEMORY GEMS

NEVER lose an opportunity to see anything beautiful.
Beauty is God's handwriting.

CHARLES KINGSLEY.

Two men look out through the same bars;
One sees the mud and one the stars.

LANGBRIDGE.

Habit is a cable; we weave the thread of it every day,
and at last we cannot break it.

HORACE MANN.

We can do more good by being good than in any
other way.

EDWARD ROWLAND SILL.

One example is worth a thousand arguments.

GLADSTONE.

There is no happiness in the whole world into which
love does not enter.

ANONYMOUS.

Then what will you sow, my dear children, what will
　　you sow?
Seeds of kindness, of sweetness, of patience, drop softly,
　　and lo!
Love shall blossom around you in joy and in beauty, and
　　make
A garden of Paradise here upon earth for your sake.
CELIA THAXTER.

Sleep, soldiers! still in honored rest
　　Your truth and valor wearing;
The bravest are the tenderest—
　　The loving are the daring.
BAYARD TAYLOR.

Though the mills of God grind slowly,
　　Yet they grind exceeding small;
Though with patience he stands waiting
　　With exactness, grinds he all.
LONGFELLOW.

Who gives himself with his alms feeds three,—
Himself, his hungering neighbor, and Me.
J. R. LOWELL.

Now the bright morning star, Day's harbinger,
Comes dancing from the East, and leads with her
The flowery May, who from her green lap throws
The yellow cowslip and the pale primrose.
MILTON.

If I were a cobbler, I'd make it my pride,
  The best of all cobblers to be;
If I were a tinker, no tinker beside
  Could mend an old kettle like me.

If I can stop one heart from breaking,
  I shall not live in vain:
If I can ease one life the aching,
  Or cool one pain,
Or help one fainting robin
  Unto his nest again,
I shall not live in vain.

EMILY DICKINSON.

If the whole world were put into one scale and my
Mother into the other, the world could not outweigh her.

LANGDALE.

Out of the bosom of the air,
  Out of the cloud-folds of her garments shaken,
Over the woodlands brown and bare,
  Over the harvest fields forsaken,
Silent and soft and slow
  Descends the snow.

LONGFELLOW.

He conquers who conquers himself.

MARY W. WILLIAMS.

" Step by step we mount the ladder,"
    Doth the Turkish proverb read;
And a double truth it teaches
    To the one who stops to heed.

Fear you not, nor faint, nor falter
    As life's steps you seek to scale;
He who constant climbs, though slowly,
    Cannot of his purpose fail.
                    Boys' Brigade Courier.

He who does faithfully today will be wanted to-morrow
                                        PROVERB.

There is very little trouble
    That happens us today.
It's the sorrow of to-morrow
    That drives our joys away.

We sometimes sit and wonder
    And stew and fume and fret
For fear something may happen,
    But it hasn't happened yet.

It's what thee'll spend, my son, not what thee'll make,
that will decide whether thee's to be rich or not.

Fortunately what God expects of us is not *the* best,
but *our* best.
                    ALICE WELLINGTON ROLLINS.

On, bravely, through the sunshine and the showers!
Time hath his work to do, and we have ours.

A loving heart is the beginning of all knowledge.

The only way to have a friend is to be one.

[From *Cymbeline*.]

Hark! hark! the lark at heaven's gate sings,
    And Phœbus 'gins arise,
His steeds to water at those springs
    On chalic'd flowers that lies;
And winking Mary-buds begin
    To ope their golden eyes:
With everything that pretty is,
    My lady sweet, arise!
                Arise, Arise!

SHAKESPEARE.

Speaking without thinking is shooting without aiming.

Better to feel a love within
    Than be lovely to the sight!
Better a homely tenderness
    Than beauty's wild delight!

MACDONALD.

Among the pitfalls in our way,
    The best of us walk blindly;
So, man, be wary, watch and pray,
    And judge your brother kindly.

ALICE CARY.

To be rich in friends is to be poor in nothing.
LILIAN WHITING.

To make a quarrel needs, indeed, two; but to make peace needs only one.
IVAN PANIN.

When you are an anvil, hold you still.
When you are a hammer, strike your fill.
Sixteenth Century Sayings.

Silence is a great peacemaker.
LONGFELLOW.

A prudent man is like a pin; his head prevents him from going too far.
DOUGLAS JERROLD.

Whosoever acquires knowledge and does not practise it resembles him who ploughs his land and leaves it unsown.
SADI.

He that spares when he is young may spend when he is old.

Be sure you are right, then go ahead.
DAVY CROCKETT.

No man was ever known to get a cent's worth without paying in some form or other the cent.

Beware of borrowing; it bringeth care by night and disgrace by day.

HINDOO.

Be true if you would be believed.

The language denotes the man.

An honest countenance is the best passport.

God's best gift to us is that he gives not things, but opportunities.

ALICE WELLINGTON ROLLINS.

MEMORY GEMS

L IFE is a leaf of paper white
  Whereon each one of us may write
His word or two; and then comes night.

Though thou have time
But for a line, be that sublime;
Not failure, but low aim, is crime.
                    JAMES RUSSELL LOWELL.

Let not one look of Fortune cast you down;
She were not Fortune if she did not frown.
                    ORREBY.

A man has no more right to say an uncivil thing than
to act one, no more right to say a rude thing to another
than to knock him down.
                    BEN JONSON.

In the grammar of life the great verbs are " To be "
and " To do."
                    STUART.

To have what we want is riches; but to be able to do
without is power.

GEORGE MACDONALD.

Have little care that life is brief,
  And less that art is long,
Success is in the silences
  Though fame is in the song.

CHRISTINA ROSSETTI.

Perseverance is a great element of success. If you
only knock long enough and loud enough at the gate,
you are sure to wake up somebody.

LONGFELLOW.

Never mention to me the word " trouble "! Only
tell me how the thing is to be done, to be done rightly,
and I will do it if I can.

VICTORIA TO LORD MONTEAGLE.

AN OPEN FIRE

For ages, dreaming in the coal,
Has slept in earth the shining soul
Which waking brings to winter's night
Some ancient summer's warmth and light.

FRANK DEMPSTER SHERMAN.

Hitch your wagon to a star.

EMERSON.

If what from far appeared so grand,
Turns to nothing in thy hand;
On again! the virtue lies
In the struggle, not the prize.

He who does not improve today will grow worse
to-morrow.   GERMAN.

Onward, onward may we press
     Through the path of duty;
Virtue is true happiness.
     Excellence true beauty.

           MONTGOMERY.

Oh, beautiful and grand,
My own, my Native Land!
     Of thee I boast;
Great Empire of the West,
The dearest and the best,
Made up of all the rest,
     I love thee most.

           COLES.

Knowledge is the hill which few may hope to climb;
Duty is the path that all may tread.

           MORRIS.

The glance that doth thy neighbor doubt
     Turn thou, O man, within,
And see if it will not bring out
     Some unsuspected sin.

           ALICE CARY.

Once to every man and nation comes the moment to decide,
In the strife of Truth with Falsehood, for the good or
   evil side.

JAMES RUSSELL LOWELL.

Sow love, and taste its fruitage pure;
   Sow peace, and reap its harvest bright;
Sow sunbeams on the rock and moor,
   And find a harvest-home of light.

BONAR.

So nigh is grandeur to our dust,
   So near is God to man,
When duty whispers low, " Thou must,"
   The youth replies, " I can."

EMERSON.

Thoughtlessness is never an excuse for wrong-doing.
Our hasty actions disclose, as nothing else does, our
habitual feeling.

Let me go where'er I will,
I hear a sky-born music still:
It is not only in the rose,
   It is not only in the bird,
Not only where the rainbow glows,
   Nor in the song of woman heard,
But in the darkest, meanest things
There always, always, something sings.

EMERSON.

Build today, then, strong and sure,
    With a firm and ample base;
And, ascending and secure,
    Shall to-morrow find its place.

                                    LONGFELLOW.

I know not where his islands lift
    Their fronded palms in air,
I only know I cannot drift
    Beyond his loving care.

                                    WHITTIER.

Strive; yet do not promise,
    The prize you dream of today,
May fade when you think to grasp it,
    And melt in your hand away;
But another and holier treasure,
    You at first perchance disdain,
Will come when your toil is over,
    And pay you for all your pain.

                        ADELAIDE A. PROCTER.

Be such a man, live such a life, that if every man
were such as you, and every life a life like yours, this
earth would be a paradise.

                                PHILLIPS BROOKS.

" Out of the lowest depth there is a path to the loftiest
height."

            Be, and not seem.

                                    EMERSON.

" A good cause makes a stout heart and a strong arm."

" Work is given to men not only . . . because the world needs it, but because the workman needs it. Work makes men."

" A man may have a just esteem of himself without being proud."

" Better lose a jest than a friend."

" Truth shall spring out of the earth; and righteousness shall look down from heaven."

" The blessing comes when we have forgotten the service rendered."

" A little knowledge is a dangerous thing."
" He that imagines he hath knowledge enough hath none."

" We keep the best things when we give them to others."

" He is not a good soldier who fights with his tongue."

An honest man is the noblest work of God.
POPE.

" When one borrows, one cannot choose."

" Want others to have the best and you will have the blessing."

" By jumping at the stars you may fall in the mud."

> In the suburb, in the town,
>   On the railway, in the square,
> Came a beam of goodness down
>   Doubling daylight everywhere:
> Peace now each for malice takes
>   Beauty for his sinful deeds,
> For the angel Hope aye makes
>   Him an angel whom she leads.
>
> EMERSON.

MEMORY GEMS

IN the lexicon of youth, which Fate reserves
For a bright manhood, there is no such word as fail.
BULWER.

What is it to be a gentleman? It is to be honest, to
be gentle, to be generous, to be brave, to be wise; and,
possessing all these qualities, to exercise them in the most
graceful outward manner.
THACKERAY.

Your manners are always under examination, and by
committees little suspected,—a police in citizen's clothes,—
but are rewarding or denying you very high prizes when
you least think of it.
EMERSON.

"The imprudent man reflects on what he has said; the
wise man on what he is going to say."

Not to go back is somewhat to advance,
And men must walk, at least, before they dance.
POPE.

" Work for some good, be it ever so slowly;
Cherish some flower, be it ever so lowly;
Labor!—all labor is noble and holy;
Let thy great deed be thy prayer to thy God."

Rest is not quitting
The busy career;
Rest is the fitting
Of self to one's sphere.

GOETHE.

He spoils his house and throws his pains away
Who as the sun veers, builds his windows o'er,
For, should he wait, the Light, some time of day,
Would come and sit beside him in his door.

ALICE CARY.

'Tis education forms the common mind;
Just as the twig is bent the tree's inclined.

POPE.

New occasions teach new duties; Time makes ancient good
uncouth;
They must upward still, and onward, who would keep
abreast of Truth.

JAMES RUSSELL LOWELL.

Do good by stealth, and blush to find it fame.

POPE.

What is excellent,
As God lives, is permanent.

EMERSON.

He who serves men, serveth few;
He serves all who dares be true.

EMERSON.

" Stainless soldier on the walls,
    Knowing this,—and knows no more,—
Whoever fights, whoever falls,
    Justice conquers evermore.

He who battles on her side,
    God, though he were ten times slain,
Crowns him victor glorified,
    Victor over death and pain."

BEAUTY

" If eyes were made for seeing,
Then Beauty is its own excuse for being.
    Why thou wert there O rival of the rose,
I never thought to ask, I never knew,
But, in my simple ignorance, suppose
    The self-same Power that brought me there brought
      you."

Trifles make perfection, and perfection is no trifle.

MICHAEL ANGELO.

" Every man's task is his life-preserver."

" Who has no time, yet waits for time, comes to a time of repentance."

" We grow as long as we give and do."

" Borrowing is the mother of trouble."

Behold what a great matter a little fire kindleth.

ST. PAUL.

Pride goeth before destruction and an haughty spirit before a fall.

PROVERBS.

" It is more necessary to guard the mouth than the chest."

Our adventures hover round us like bees round the hive when preparing to swarm.

MAETERLINCK.

And whether you climb up the mountain or go down the hill to the valley, whether you journey to the end of the world or merely walk round your house, none but yourself shall you meet on the highway of fate.

MAETERLINCK.

The lives of men who have been always growing, are strewed along their whole course with the things they have learned to do without.

PHILLIPS BROOKS.

" The motive gives the quality to the act."

Self-denial is painful for the moment, but very agreeable in the end.

JANE TAYLOR.

" Be sensitive for others and you will forget to be sensitive for yourself."

Reading maketh a full man, conversation a ready man. and writing an exact man.

LORD BACON.

" A man is never so noble as when he is reverent."

" He who does a good deed is instantly ennobled.
" He who does a mean deed is by the action itself contracted."

" He that would jest must take a jest,
Else to let it alone is best."

The wisest man could ask no more of Fate,
Than to be modest, manly and true,
Safe from the many, honored by the few.

LOWELL.

Let lands and houses have what lords they will,
Let us be fixed and our own masters still.

POPE.

What, and how great the virtue and the art,
To live on little with a cheerful heart.

POPE.

Nature is a revelation of God;
Art a revelation of man.

LONGFELLOW.

I will be lord over myself. No one who cannot master
himself is worthy to rule, and only he can rule.

GOETHE.

Nature ever faithful is
To such as trust her faithfulness.

EMERSON.

" On the whole we make too much of faults;
Faults? The greatest of faults, I should say, is to have
none."

Knowledge comes, but wisdom lingers.

TENNYSON.

Wisdom is the principal thing; therefore get wisdom,
and with all thy getting get understanding.

PROVERBS IV:7.

Ignorance is the curse of God,
Knowledge the wing wherewith we fly to Heaven.

SHAKESPEARE.

In books lies the soul of the whole past time.

CARLYLE.

Words are also actions and actions are a kind of words.

EMERSON.

There is but one temple in the universe, and that is the body of man.

NOVALIS.

As one lamp lights another, nor grows less,
So nobleness enkindleth nobleness.

JAMES RUSSELL LOWELL.

Art is long and time is fleeting.

LONGFELLOW.

The history of the world is the biography of great men.

CARLYLE.

Memory is the treasurer and guardian of all things.

CICERO.

Beauty is the creator of the universe.

EMERSON.

The great secret of success in life is for a man to be ready when his opportunity comes.

LORD BEACONSFIELD.

Much tongue and much judgment seldom go together.

L'ESTRANGE.

" We shall find the Grail when we can use it."

Procrastination is the thief of time;
Year after year it steals till all are fled.

YOUNG.

Exaggeration is to paint a snake and to add legs.

CHINESE PROVERB.

Courage in danger is half the battle.

PLAUTUS.

" Too much humility is pride."

" Difficulties exist to be surmounted.   Failure is part of
success.   A man's success is made up of failures."

MEMORY GEMS

THERE is a tide in the affairs of men,
    Which, taken at the flood, leads on to fortune;
Omitted, all the voyage of their life
Is bound in shallows and in miseries.
On such a full sea are we now afloat;
And we must take the current when it serves,
Or lose our ventures.

SHAKESPEARE.

Tact is the life of five senses. It is the open eye, the quick ear, the judging taste, the keen touch. Talent is power, tact is skill; talent is weight, tact is momentum; talent knows what to do, tact how to do it; talent is wealth, tact ready money.

London Atlas.

" Sow an act, and you reap a habit;
    Sow a habit, and you reap character;
    Sow a character, and you reap a destiny."

Too low they build who build beneath the stars.

YOUNG.

Experience shows that success is due less to ability than to zeal. The winner is he who gives himself to his work, body and soul.

BUXTON.

Flower in the crannied wall,
I pluck you out of the crannies;
Hold you here, root and all, in my hand,
Little flower—but if I could understand
What you are, root and all, all in all,
I should know what God and man is.

TENNYSON.

Who builds a church to God, and not to fame,
Will never mark the marble with his name.

POPE.

One self-approving hour whole years outweighs
Of stupid starers and of loud huzzas.

POPE.

One all-extending, all-preserving soul
Connects each being, greatest with the least;
Made beast in aid of man, and man in aid of beast;
All served, all serving; nothing stands alone;
The chain holds on and where it ends unknown.

POPE.

Order is heaven's first law, and this confest,
Some are, and must be, greater than the rest.

POPE.

How happy is he born or taught
  Who serveth not another's will;
Whose armor is his honest thought,
  And simple truth his highest skill.
                    SIR HENRY WOTTON.

This above all, to thine own self be true,
And it must follow, as the night the day,
Thou canst not then be false to any man.
                        SHAKESPEARE.

Vice is a monster of so frightful mien,
As, to be hated, needs but to be seen;
Yet seen too oft, familiar with her face,
We first endure, then pity, then embrace.
                                POPE.

Annual income, £20; annual expenses, £19 19s 6d—
result, happiness.

Annual income, £20; annual expenses, £20, 0s 6d—
result, misery.

                        DICKENS.

It takes far less insight to discover defects than it
does to discern noble and lovely qualities. "It requires
a god to recognize a god."

                        LILIAN WHITING.

Life is work . . . Life without work is unworthy
of being lived.

                    BISHOP BICKERSTETH.

Finish every day and be done with it. You have done what you could; some blunders and absurdities crept in; forget them as soon as you can. To-morrow is a new day; you shall begin it well and serenely and with too high a spirit to be encumbered with your old nonsense.

EMERSON.

" There is no beautifier of complexion or form or behavior like the wish to scatter joy, and not pain, around us."

" There is nothing more precious than time and nothing more prodigally wasted."

" They that make the best use of their time have none to spare."

The battle of life extends over a vast area, and it is vain for us to inquire about the other wings of the army; it is enough that we have received our orders, and that we have held the few feet of ground committed to our charge.

IAN MACLAREN.

Every famous life is raised upon the lives of others, as a Venetian palace rests upon the piles beneath the water.

IAN MACLAREN.

Oh, there is no man, no woman, so small that they cannot make their life great by high endeavor.

CARLYLE.

Neither a borrower nor a lender be,
For loan oft loses both itself and friend.

SHAKESPEARE.

Honesty is the best policy; but he who acts on that
principle is not an honest man.

ARCHBISHOP WHATELY.

You must live each day at your very best;
The work of the world is done by few,
God asks that a part be done by you.

SARAH H. BOLTON.

When a strong brain is weighed with a true heart, it
seems to be like balancing a bubble against a wedge of
gold.

HOLMES.

Be firm; one constant element in luck
Is genuine, solid, old Teutonic pluck.

HOLMES.

Manner maketh man, and a pleasing figure is a per-
petual letter of recommendation.

BACON.

A great part of the happiness in life consists not in
fighting battles, but in avoiding them. A masterly retreat
is in itself a victory.

LONGFELLOW.

There is no duty, the fulfilment of which will not make you happier, nor any temptation for which there is no remedy.

SENECA.

Think naught a trifle, though it small appear,
Small sands the mountain, moments make the year,
And trifles life.

YOUNG.

The first creature of God was the light of sense; the last was the light of reason.

BACON.

Only the actions of the just smell sweet and blossom in the dust.

JAMES SHIRLEY.

Science is organized knowledge.

HERBERT SPENCER.

Beauty is truth, truth beauty.

KEATS.

Man raises, but time weighs.

GREEK PROVERB.

There is no work of genius which has not been the delight of mankind.

JAMES RUSSELL LOWELL.

Beneath the rule of men entirely great
The pen is mightier than the sword.

BULWER LYTTON.

The noblest motive is the public good.

VIRGIL.

A little learning is a dangerous thing;
Drink deep or taste not the Pierian spring.

POPE.

Studies perfect nature and are perfected by experience.

BACON.

One God, one law, one element,
And one far off divine event,
To which the whole creation moves.

TENNYSON.

Of law there can be no less acknowledged than that
her voice is the harmony of the world.

HOOKER.

The heavens declare the glory of God; and the firmament sheweth his handiwork.

PSALM XIX:I.

It is the mind that makes the man, and our vigor is
in our immortal soul.

OVID.

They are never alone that are accompanied with noble thoughts.

Sir Philip Sydney.

Tongues in trees, books in the running brooks,
Sermons in stones, and good in everything.

Shakespeare.

Books will speak plain when counsellors blanch.

Bacon.

Glory is acquired by virtue, but preserved by letters.

Petrarch.

The foundation of every state is the education of its youth.

Dionysius.

The light shineth in darkness, and the darkness comprehended it not.

St. John 1:5.

The true University of these days is a Collection of Books.

Carlyle.

Nature is the art of God.

Sir Thomas Browne.

Beholding the bright countenance of Truth in the quiet and still air of delightful studies.

Milton.

Ill fares the land, to hastening ills a prey,
Where wealth accumulates and men decay:
Princes and lords may flourish, or may fade;
A breath can make them, as a breath has made:
But a bold peasantry, their country's pride,
When once destroyed, can never be supplied.

GOLDSMITH.

THE END